THE CHURCH FAMILY SINGS

SONGS, IDEAS, AND ACTIVITIES FOR USE IN CHURCH SCHOOL

Anne Streaty Wimberly

Abingdon Press
Nashville

THE CHURCH FAMILY SINGS
Songs, Ideas, and Activities for Use in Church School

Copyright © 1996 by Abingdon Press

This book is printed on acid-free, recycled paper.

ISBN 0-687-02085-9

96 97 98 99 00 01 02 03 04 05 — 10 9 8 7 6 5 4 3 2 1

MANUFACTURED IN THE UNITED STATES OF AMERICA

**To my mother
Mrs. Valeska B. Streaty**

CONTENTS

PREFACE

This is a book of songs, ideas, and activities for you! Whether you are a church school or vacation Bible school leader or teacher, Bible study group leader, camp or retreat leader, choir director, family worship leader, or someone who just loves to sing, the songs, ideas, and activities included in this volume are for your use. You are invited to use what you find here to bring about your own and others' enjoyment of music and further learning about the Christian faith through singing and creative involvement.

The book builds on two important understandings. First, music is a vital part of Christian education and Christian life. Christians past and present claim it as a great gift from God and admit that it is hard to imagine a people of God without music. Second, people can use music readily and creatively in church schools, vacation Bible schools, Bible study groups, camps, choirs, and families when there are helpful guides and resources.

Several things stimulated me to develop this resource. First, I love music! I love to sing! Second, music was a big part of what made church and family times come alive as I grew up. Third, among my greatest joys have been opportunities over many years for me to bring music to young people in schools and to God's people in local churches. Finally, the stimulus for writing the book came most particularly from my more recent years of experiences with church school music students at the Interdenominational Theological Center, and with my intergenerational church school class at Rocky Head United Methodist Church, Atlanta, Georgia. In both of these arenas, I have had the privilege of presenting and experimenting with songs, ideas, and activities to make music come alive in church and family.

Our experiences together in seminary and church school classes confirmed something very important. We discovered over and over again the power music can have on our lives as Christians. As we sang new songs, explored where they came from, considered why singing them was important, and studied scriptures with which songs related, we found ourselves being brought together like family. We found ourselves being renewed. We learned new things about ourselves and the Christian faith. We were enriched communally, educationally, and spiritually. My hope is that the songs, ideas, and activities in the book will generate this kind of outcome for you.

The use of movement, instruments, the related arts, and games with my groups continued to remind us of the many doors to self-expression music opens. We discovered that music stimulates the creative self and awakens still more possibilities for creative expression. My hope is that the activities in this book will open these same doors for you and those with whom you use this resource.

I am indebted to many students for their insights that came from "trying out" songs, ideas, and activities both in our classes together and in groups they led. Their willing efforts helped me to see infinitely more possibilities than I would have seen otherwise. I am also indebted to Mrs. Pamela Jones and Ms. Tamara Battice for the time they took to review various parts of the book, suggest songs, offer helpful critical comments, and encourage me "to get on with it." And, I am indebted to my husband, Edward, and my mother, Mrs. Valeska Streaty, who were affirming presences during the process of completing all that you find here.

INTRODUCTION
AN INVITATION TO SING

An Example

As the children entered their church school room, the teacher greeted them and quickly drew them into a circle, saying, "Let's sing!" They sang a good morning song. They sang several of the children's favorite songs. They sang a prayer. They retold a Bible story they had learned in song. They clapped their hands, tapped their feet, held hands, and moved in the circle as they sang. They acted out the Bible story. They smiled. They giggled. They said, "This is fun! Let's do it again!" The teacher smiled. The teacher giggled! The teacher said, "I think it's fun, too. Yes, we will do it again!"

Know What It Means to Invite

When we invite church school or other church-related groups to sing, we create for them the opportunity for a unique shared experience. Our invitation means we are ready to make way for music! We are ready to welcome it! We are determined to "find a musical way" of exploring and expressing who we are as Christians.

We extend our welcome to come together in song because we know that singing brings vitality to what we are doing. We see its vitality in the opening story. When we invite singing, we bring about this same vitality, regardless of the age/stage, size of group, or church context. Through our invitation, we confirm that music is for everybody!

Prepare to Make It Happen

Inviting groups to sing requires knowing what music has to offer that can enliven what we do. It requires knowing what it offers that supports the goal of Christian education. Let us take a moment to think about what is unique about singing songs that makes us want our groups to do it. And, let us consider our role in making it happen.

Singing Has Special Functions

Singing songs is a participatory, creative, expressive, enriching, and instructional art. It captures our attention. It engages us individually and in groups. We express ourselves through it in ways not otherwise possible. It makes us feel good. We teach and learn things about human experience and Christian life through it. It is hard to imagine life without music.

Because of its special functions, singing songs can make a unique contribution to the activities we plan for our church school participants. What are these functions? How can music function in ways that assist us in carrying out our purpose of Christian education in which all church groups participate?

Consider the following five functions:

1. Singing songs can contribute to our enjoyment.
2. Singing songs can be a catalyst for community formation.
3. Singing songs of many cultures can raise our awareness of our human diversity and differing ways of expressing the Christian faith.
4. Singing songs can remind us of Bible stories and truths and can make possible our rehearsing these stories and truths in creative ways.
5. Singing songs can extend our understanding of Christian church traditions and can make possible our creative expression of them.

These five functions of singing are important for vital church group experiences. They are important because they can help us carry out the primary goal of Christian education in the church school. Our goal is to enable participants to deepen their understanding of the Christian faith in ways that free their discovery of how to express that faith in community with love, hope, courage, and integrity. We want to make the Christian faith come alive in our participants' hearts, minds, and actions. We do this in a variety of ways. Singing songs is one of those ways.

In the following sections of this book, we will use the five functions of singing to explore ways of making music a vital part of activities with church groups. This means we will explore ways we can help our groups (1) sing for joy, (2) sing songs to build community, (3) sing songs from many cultures, (4) tell Bible stories through song, and (5) tell about church traditions through song. We will see examples of how it has been done in the church school. We will look at what it means to do it. We will explore how to make it happen through actual songs.

The Leader/Teacher Makes It Happen

Vital use of music with church groups depends greatly on us as leaders/teachers. We are most likely to create excitement and involvement in our groups when we feel at ease with music, enjoy it, and desire to share it. Sometimes, however, leaders/teachers think they can't do it because they say, "I can't carry a tune in a bucket," or "I don't know what to do with a song beyond just singing it." Yet, when these leaders/teachers discover approaches that really work, they feel freed and energized to make music happen where they are. The final chapter in this book is designed to give eight easy approaches to presenting songs in the church school—to leaders/teachers who sing, and to those who think they cannot sing.

So, let's get started! Let the church family sing!

1. SING FOR JOY

An Example

*M*s. J leads an intermediate church school group. She described her group as a "dynamo of energy." But, she also said that "their energy gets channeled in creative ways through music. Music really taps their interest and, besides, they have great talent and ideas for what to do." So, she plans for her group with music interspersed throughout. She said, "The group sings songs to get started. Songs give us a change of pace at different points. Songs help to wind things up just right. We sing praise songs, favorite songs, songs that tell how we feel and what we believe, songs that connect with something we're studying. We use instruments, tapes, and movement. We make up rhythms with hand claps, toe taps, and finger snaps. We make up our own songs and raps."

Ms. J went on, "I remember one time when we were on a six-week study unit, we started the first session with praise songs. At the end of the session, I gave the study topic and the scripture for the next session. After giving it, the group members and I named songs we knew that related to the topic to begin our next session. I also asked volunteers to create a rap song. We decided on three songs and one rap, after discussing why we thought they related to the topic.

"I encouraged group members to present the songs and involve their peers in a variety of ways. I gave them some suggestions. For example, I told them they may comment on what the song and rap are saying and what they mean to them. They may use rhythm instruments for accompaniment. They may also ask another group member or friend to play the piano or another instrument to accompany the songs. Or they may ask several group members to sing particular verses. I was surprised that they did all of these things and more. One group member audiotaped a song she sang with her mother, accompanied by piano and violin played by another mother and group member. And, three group members formed a group they called The Jesus Rappers. We ended up doing something like this for every session of the six-week unit.

"My group sings songs because they love to sing. It's enjoyable. I can tell, it makes everybody feel good." Ms. J went on, "Now, I'll have to say that I'm not the best singer in the world. But, I'll admit, I enjoy it too. And, because I get all excited about it, they get excited. I mean, there's nothing stopping us, not even my voice."

Know What It Means to Sing for Joy

One way we can make the Christian faith come alive in the church school and other church-related groups is to lead the groups in singing songs of the faith for the joy these songs bring. We stimulate joyful participation by awakening our participants' interests in singing and by engaging them in experiences of singing. When we lead groups in singing songs of the faith, we make possible their expression of thoughts, feelings, and beliefs that are often difficult to express in other ways. We can say in song what we feel deeply. Singing it makes us feel good. It brings us more joy when we're happy. It helps move us from sadness to joy. We can tell in song what we already know about the Christian faith, what we are learning about it, and how we have lived and intend to live it. Telling about the Christian faith in song can make us feel good. It can give us joy.

We affirm our beliefs when we sing songs reflecting them. Singing gives us an opportunity to hear ourselves express what we believe and to say in our hearts, "Yes! This is what I stand for!" This kind of expression makes us feel good. It gives us joy.

Singing is an experience of the whole self. It can inspire hand claps, foot taps, finger snaps, body swaying, pantomiming, dramatizing, or playing musical instruments. The message and mood of songs can prompt quiet tones and a prayerful attitude. We can also be moved to create songs. To be involved in these ways can make us feel good. It can bring us joy.

How to Make It Happen

Suggested songs to sing for joy appear on upcoming pages with ideas and activities for their use. Some general guidelines include the following:

- Begin and end with singing. Use songs that emphasize the act of singing and that lend themselves to movement, drama, games, and other creative activities.
- Choose songs of praise to God.
- Choose songs that tell about Christian ideals and values such as faith, hope, love, peace, justice, and reconciliation.
- Choose songs that tell about the work of the Holy Spirit.
- Invite group members to create their own songs and rap music.
- When there is a strong song leader, don't hesitate to sing without accompaniment. But, don't hesitate, either, to use instrumental accompaniment by calling on anyone who can play. For example: piano, guitar, autoharp, ukelele, bells, harmonica, recorder, drums, or a

brass, wind, or stringed orchestral instrument may be used.

- Have an array of rhythm instruments for use with songs and rap music. These might include:
- Use songs that relate to units of study or for group and individual reflection. Ask group members to help choose the songs and to suggest and show ways of presenting them.

Rhythm Sticks

Triangles

Jingle Bells

Cymbals

Tambourines

Drums

Sandblocks

Woodblocks

Maracas or Rattles

- If no commercial rhythm instruments are available, have group members create them. The following directions may be used:

Sticks:
Use twelve-inch dowel pins. Sand and paint the dowel lengths.

Triangle:
Use a horseshoe or a length of rolled steel suspended by a cord and struck with a large nail.

Jingle Bells:
Cut 8" x 1" strips of colored cloth or plastic. Sew on three bells. Make a bracelet by stapling the ends of the cloth or plastic together. To play the jin-

gle bells, put the bracelet on the wrist and shake it.

Cymbals:
Use two large aluminum pot lids of equal size. To play the cymbals, strike the two lids together by bringing one in an upward motion and the other in a downward motion.

Tambourine:
Place the rims of two aluminum pie tins or plastic foam plates together after putting pebbles or beans inside them. Punch five holes an equal distance apart through both rims. Punch a hole in the center of ten flattened soda bottle caps. Attach two bottle caps closely but not snugly to each of the five holes in the rims with colored ribbons or string. Use colored markers to decorate the tambourine. To play the tambourine, shake it and hit the sides.

Drum:
For big drums, use empty barrels or gallon cans turned upside down with a circle of denim pasted on the side to be struck. For small drums, use oatmeal or cornmeal boxes, or canister-type cans (coffee or shortening cans) with plastic covers. Cover the cans with construction paper and decorate with colored markers or crayon. Use twelve-inch dowel pins for drum sticks, or make mallets by attaching a circular piece of cloth to a dish mop with a string.

Sandblocks:
Cover the bottoms and sides of two small blocks of wood with sandpaper. Screw in two knobs (the kind used for drawer pulls). To play them, rub the two covered blocks together.

Woodblocks:
Use the wooden side of two wooden chalkboard erasers. To play the woodblocks, strike the wooden sides together.

Maracas or Rattles:
Place beans or pebbles in a small baking powder can with a plastic top. Paste construction paper around the can and decorate with brightly colored markers or crayon. To play the maracas or rattles, simply shake them.

Let Us Sing Together

Four-part Round

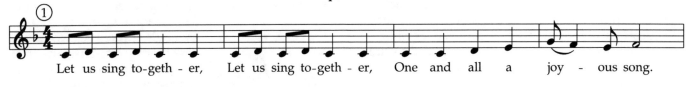

Let us sing to-geth - er, Let us sing to-geth - er, One and all a joy - ous song.

Let us sing to - geth - er, One and all a joy - ous song.

Let us sing a - gain and a - gain, Let us sing a - gain and a - gain,

Let us sing a - gain and a - gain, One and all a joy - ous song.

WORDS: Traditional
MUSIC: Adapted from a Czech folk tune

Activities

1. Sing the song several times or until everyone is very familiar with it. Then sing the song as a four-part round. To do this, find the numbers 1, 2, 3, and 4 in the song. These numbers indicate four different groups of singers (or parts). The location of these numbers tells when each group's part should begin. It is helpful when singing the round for the first time to use only two groups. Add groups 3 and 4 gradually.

2. Choose people for each of the four groups to sing the song as a round. Have everyone read Psalm 146:1-2 before singing the song together. Continue by having Group 2 read Psalm 147:1 before singing the song as a two-part round. Continue by having Group 3 read Psalm 149:1 before singing the song as a three-part round. Continue by having Group 4 read Psalm 150:1-2 before singing the song as a four-part round.

This Is the Reason Why I Sing

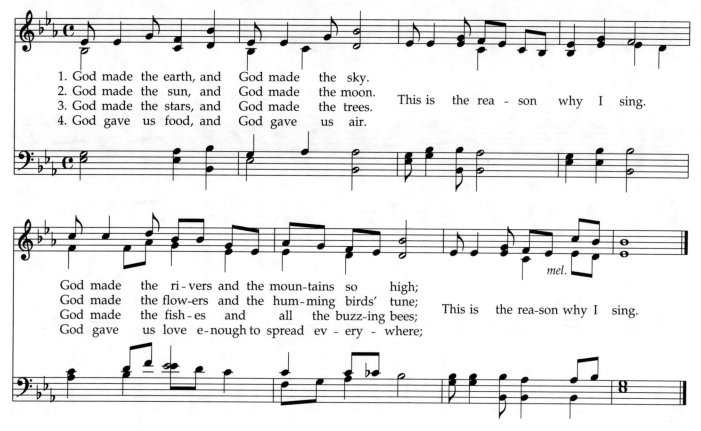

WORDS and MUSIC: Anne Wimberly

Activities

1. Before singing the song, have group members name all the things they can think of that God has made.

2. Have the group learn the song and dramatize it through hand and body motions.

3. Draw a picture poster with the title of the song on it, and picture posters showing all of the things God made in the order they appear in the song. Then make a videotape of the pictures, with the group singing the song in the background. Appoint a narrator to begin the video with the words, "This is a video that tells the reason why we sing." The narrator may then say words that begin the story of creation: "Long ago, before time began, our world was dark and desolate. Then God began to create order and beauty."[1]

4. Have someone play the following bell part or have part of the group sing the notes on the syllable "oo."

Sing for Joy!

WORDS and MUSIC: Lois Horton Young

Activities

1. Accompany this song on piano, guitar, or other instrument.

2. Have selected members of the group create a dance to the song using brightly colored scarves.

Praise God in the Morning

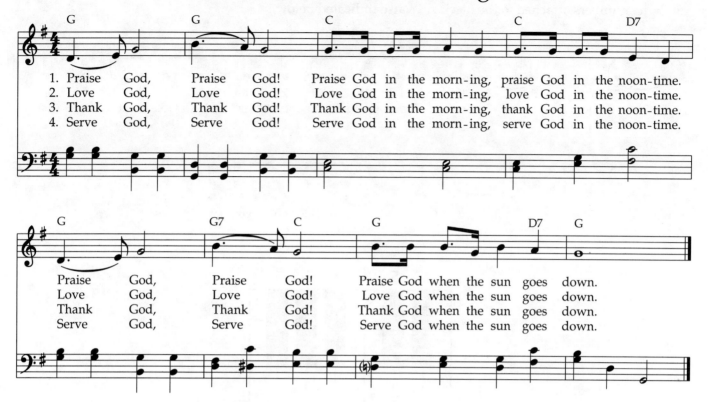

1. Praise God, Praise God! Praise God in the morn-ing, praise God in the noon-time.
2. Love God, Love God! Love God in the morn-ing, love God in the noon-time.
3. Thank God, Thank God! Thank God in the morn-ing, thank God in the noon-time.
4. Serve God, Serve God! Serve God in the morn-ing, serve God in the noon-time.

Praise God, Praise God! Praise God when the sun goes down.
Love God, Love God! Love God when the sun goes down.
Thank God, Thank God! Thank God when the sun goes down.
Serve God, Serve God! Serve God when the sun goes down.

For a lighter piano accompaniment, play only the lower note of each chord in the left-hand part.

WORDS: Psalm 113:1-3
MUSIC: Traditional chorus

Activities

1. Use the song to introduce or summarize a discussion on who God is and appreciation of what God does.

2. The verses of the song connect in various ways with Psalm 113:1-4 (Praise God); Psalm 116:1-2 (Love God); Psalm 92:1-4 (Thank God); and Psalm 100:1-2 (Serve God). In one group session, focus on only one verse of the song and the scripture passage that connects with it. Invite the group to share why it is important to do what the song verse tells us to do. Also ask the group to share how they may carry out what the verses say in the morning, noon, and night (e.g., saying good morning to God each day, praying before meal times and at bedtime, being kind to others).

3. Read the scripture that connects with each verse. Ask group members to raise their hands each time they hear the same words as the beginning words of the song verses.

4. The repetitive words in the song and the five-tone (pentatonic) melody make it an easy song to teach and learn. The melody can be played on the black keys of the piano by matching the numbers appearing below with the numbers attached to the black keys also indicated below.

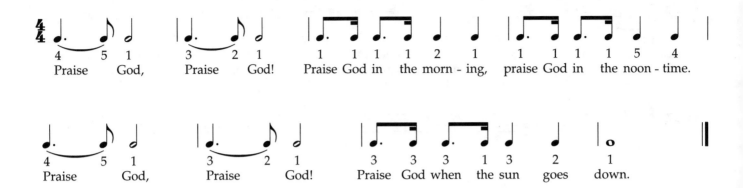

	4	5	1	3	2	1	1	1	1	1	2	1	1	1	1	1	5	4

Praise God, Praise God! Praise God in the morn - ing, praise God in the noon - time.

4 5 1   3 2 1   3 3 3 1 3 2 1

Praise God, Praise God! Praise God when the sun goes down.

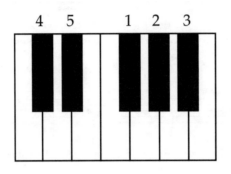

A Jesus Power Rap

Clap, then put both arms down to the side, with a striking sound, followed by a stomp with one foot and then the other.
Raise both arms and shout.

WORDS and MUSIC: Anne Streaty Wimberly

Activities

1. Ask the group to give examples of all the places and occasions they can think of where people cheer.

2. Call attention to the cheer as an example of Christian rap music. After the group learns the rap, choose someone from the group to be the leader. Or, have one half the group take the leader's part and the other half give the response.

3. Invite the group to add new words to the rap.

I'm Goin' a Sing When the Spirit Says Sing

1. I'm goin'-a *sing when the Spir - it says sing,

I'm goin'-a sing when the Spir - it says sing,

I'm goin'-a sing when the Spir - it says sing,

and o - bey the Spir - it of the Lord.

*2. pray 3. dance 4. shout

WORDS: African-American spiritual
MUSIC: African-American spiritual; adapted by William Farley Smith

Adapted © 1989 The United Methodist Publishing House. From *The United Methodist Hymnal*.

Activities

1. Clap while singing the song.

2. Have the group add verses to the song.

Alabaré
(I Will Praise My Lord)

WORDS: Traditional
MUSIC: Traditional; percussion arr. Anne Wimberly

Activities

1. Call attention to the meaning of the Spanish words.

2. Substitute clapping for the use of rhythm instruments.

2. SING SONGS TO BUILD COMMUNITY

An Example

All the church school groups entered the assembly room for forty-five minutes of community sharing. They came together following short separate group meetings to sing songs and share action ideas on the theme, "Living the Good News in the World Community."

The groups received a leaflet prepared by the assembly committee giving the meaning of the theme on which the groups had focused in preceding weeks. The leaflet said in part: "The Good News is God's love shown in Jesus Christ. We live the Good News in community when we see all people as sisters and brothers." The leaflet included scriptures for home study.

The room was decorated with three bright banners, flags, and large pictures of the world's people they had contributed. The banners contained Christian symbols.[1] The groups also heard the familiar sounds of "We Are the Church" being played on the piano as they entered.

The assembly continued with songs about building community. They read the leaflet. They learned the meanings of the banners. They heard presentations from various age groups about meanings of the songs and how they could make them come alive every day.

Know What It Means to Sing Songs to Build Community

Songs have the power to unify people. In singing together, people honor God's presence and activity in their lives and in the world. Their unified voices bring into being a common song and a shared experience of the Christian faith. Singing together confirms our unity as Christian people.

Songs can bring us together simply because we are singing them together. But, songs can also teach us about the meaning of community and our role in it as Christian disciples. Songs can affirm our differences and what we have in common. They can remind us how we are to treat one another in community. They can emphasize the exemplary love of God shown in Jesus Christ. They can inspire us to be Christian disciples in the world community.

Songs that have the power to bring us together as Christians are songs that relate us to God. These songs focus our attention on God and our unity in Christ. They tell us about the church as Christian community. They stimulate our thinking about our need to worship God together, to act both as individuals and as a whole Christian community as God's ambassadors,

and to seek God's help. The songs we choose that have these qualities are called *unity-evoking songs*. They summon us to be and to build community. They serve as prayers for God's help in doing this.

Songs teach about the meaning of community when they reveal qualities required of us as members of the Christian community. These songs focus on humankind or the family of God made up of diverse people—local, national, and global; and they center on our responsibility or the call for Christians to act out God's love by responding to human need. Through singing these songs, we rehearse and commit to making concrete the meaning of community expressed through the words. The songs we choose that have these qualities are called *community-focused songs*. They tell us how to be and to build community by highlighting the core characteristics of the Christians we intend to be in community.

Our use of both unity-evoking songs and community-focused songs is important to what we want to accomplish in the church school.

How to Make It Happen

We will explore various ideas for introducing the songs found in the opening example. Activities for their use appear underneath each song. Some general guidelines include the following:

- Introduce a song by reading aloud the words as poetry. Invite group members to close their eyes and form an image that captures what the words are saying. Ask them to share their images. Then sing the song.
- Introduce a song by asking group members to read silently and reflect on the importance of the words "we" or "us" appearing in it. Also ask them to reflect on the relationship of "we" to God. Ask group members to share their reflections. Then sing the song.
- Ask group members to share concerns for which they desire group help, support, or prayer. Use as a prayer any song that addresses God directly.
- Sing songs that highlight a lesson or scripture focused on community.
- Where possible, form a circle and sing songs while in the circle. Whether in a circle or in other seating arrangements, join hands while singing.

UNITY-EVOKING SONGS
Different Is Beautiful

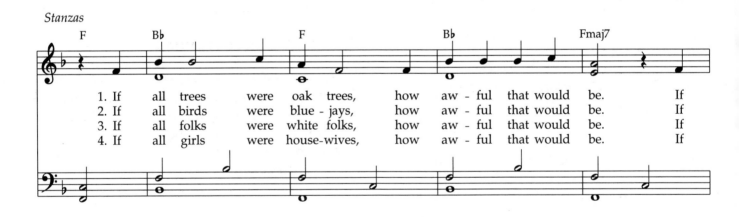

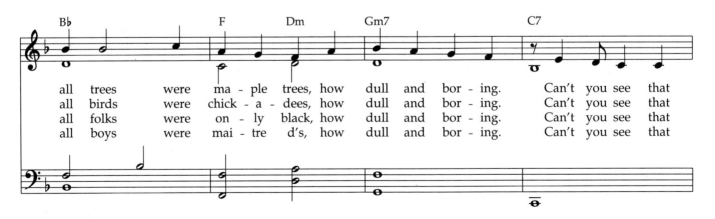

WORDS and MUSIC: Richard K. Avery and Donald S. Marsh

God made the oak and the ma - ple tree,
God made the jay and the chick - a - dee,
God made a rain - bow so - ci - e - ty,
God made the house - wife and mai - tre d',

God in great cre - a - tiv - i - ty!
God in a flight of jeu d'es - prit!
God in great in - gen - u - i - ty!
God in great lib - er - al - i - ty!

Hem - lock and beech, myr - tle, pine and yew,
Cat - bird and cow - bird and dead Do - do,
Ger - man and Turk, Tam - il, Pole and Finn;
Doc - tor, law - yer and In - dian chief,

chest - nut and peach, eu - ca - lyp - tus too,
sap - suck - er, pen - guin and vir - e - o,
short peo - ple, tall peo - ple fat and thin,
bank - er and some - one who needs re - lief,

ban - yan, ba - na - na and jun - i - per,
fly - catch - er, phoe - be and phea - sant, too,
Chi - nese, Aus - tra - lian and Cree and Sioux,
gar - bage col - lec - tor and T V star,

gin - ko and gua - va and palm and fir.
flick - er and finch and can you guess WHOOO?
hair - y and bald peo - ple me and you.
stu - dent and teach - er and what you are.

D.C. al Fine

We Are the Church

2. We're many kinds of people
   With many kinds of faces,
   All colors and all ages, too, from
   All times and and places. *(Refrain)*

3. Sometimes the church is marching,
   Sometimes it's bravely burning,
   Sometimes it's riding, sometimes hiding,
   Always it's learning. *(Refrain)*

4. And when the people gather
   There's singing and there's praying,
   There's laughing and there's crying sometimes,
   All of it saying: *(Refrain)*

5. At Pentecost some people
   Received the Holy Spirit
   And told the Good News through the world to
   All who would hear it. *(Refrain)*

6. I count if I am ninety
   Or nine, or just a baby;
   There's one thing I am sure about and
   I don't mean maybe: *(Refrain)*

* Chords are for autoharp or guitar; where alternate chords are given in parentheses, they are for guitar only.

WORDS and MUSIC: Richard K. Avery and Donald S. Marsh

Activities

1. Introduce the song as part of opening or closing worship. Begin with the refrain. Move to a prayer of praise to God for the gift of the church community and our part in it. Discuss why the song moves from "I am the church" to "We are the church."

2. Read and discuss Romans 12:4-9. Relate it to the song.

3. Explore meanings of the Pentecost story found in Acts 2:1-13. Discuss the Pentecost symbols churches use. Make a Pentecost banner or poster.

4. Form a circle and dramatize the refrain. Point both hands toward self on "I am the church." Extend both arms outward on "You are the church." Join hands on "We are the church together," and rotate the circle in a marching fashion.

5. On a long sheet of newsprint, have the group create a mural showing people who make up their local church family. Draw church people doing various tasks in church and community.

6. Discuss what the National and World Councils of Churches are and what they do. Display pictures of people at worship or in helping roles in countries around the world. Ask group members to tell what they see in the pictures that tells them about God's church as a worldwide church. Also have them explore the work of missionaries around the world.

Jesu, Jesu

WORDS: Tom Colvin
MUSIC: Ghana folk song; adapt. by Tom Colvin; arr. by Charles H. Webb

Activities

1. Begin by reading Ephesians 5:1-2. Ask group members to give sentences about what it means to be an imitator of Jesus Christ. Say the words of the refrain as a prayer. Then move from the spoken prayer to quiet drum beats as indicated above before singing the entire song.

2. Have group members place pictures of themselves, family members, and any they have of people at work, school, and play on a bulletin board or table in full view. Call attention to these pictures as God's local family members.

3. Have group members identify and list on the chalkboard or on cards the names of ethnic cultural groups, age groups, geographic groups, and socioeconomic groups that make up God's national family members.

4. Place a globe of the world on a table or hang a world map in full view. Use ribbons to connect ethnic cultural group names to the countries of their cultural heritage. Use ribbons, as well, to show where church missionaries serve. Place cards beneath the globe or map to show countries that are unfamiliar and about which the group needs further information.

5. Ask the group: "Why does God expect Christians to show love to people different in color, heritage, geographic region, age, and socioeconomic level from themselves? What does it mean to summon God for help in loving others? Why do people need to pray to be filled with the love of Jesus Christ?"

6. Ask group members to create short sentence prayers asking God to help them to help others. Ask them to do this on paper first, followed by reading them one by one. After each one, have the group respond by singing the refrain of "Jesu, Jesu."

7. Make a class prayer book with the sentence prayers they created.

8. Have group members write pledges about what they intend to do, with God's help, to be loving. Then form a circle and sing the song again as the circle rotates.

We Love

* Indicates to play wood block. ** Indicates to clap.
Woodblock may be substituted with any percussion instrument available.

WORDS: 1 John 4:19
MUSIC: Ann F. Price
ARRANGEMENT: Timothy Edmonds

Music © 1975 by Graded Press. Arrangement © 1992 by Cokesbury.

Activities

1. Explore what the word *love* means. Have the group make a list of synonyms (respect, honor, kindness, appreciation, consideration, generosity, tenderness, thoughtfulness).

2. Read and discuss the scriptures, John 3:16 and John 13:34-35. Ask the group to describe ways in which Jesus showed God's love to others. Ask them to tell how and by whom love is shown them. Also ask them to tell how and to whom they show love to others.

3. Using the synonym list, ask them: "In what new ways might you show love to persons at home, school, work, play?"

I'm Going To Teach You A New Word Today
(Peace Song)

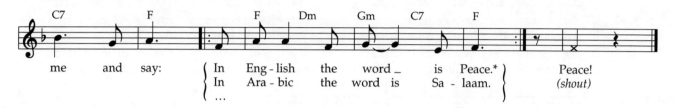

In Hebrew the word is Shalom.
In Russian the word is Meer.
In Greek the word is Irene (ih–ray–nay).
In Chinese the word is Ho Ping.
In Swahili the word is Amani.
In Japanese the word is Hey–wah.
In French the word is Paix.
In Spanish the word is Paz.
In German the word is Freide.
In Korean the word is Pyung Wah.

* This phrase is cumulative. Each time, add a new word from the list and repeat all previously sung words.
WORDS and MUSIC: Benny Berman

Activities

1. Make flash cards on which the word *peace* appears in the different languages occurring in the song. On the back side of the flash card, put the language that appears on the front of the card. Teach the words using the flash cards.

2. Sing the song. Be sure to note that the last phrase in the song is cumulative. This means that each time through, the group should add a new language from the list that is given and repeat all the previously sung languages.

3. Ask the group: "Why is peace an important characteristic of community? How is peace related to love? How may we be peacemakers at home, school, work, and play?" Have the children make "peace medallions" from construction paper by drawing, cutting, decorating circles and printing the word *peace* in the center. When finished, pin the medallions on the collar.

4. Invite the group to play the following matching game:
Draw a line from the word on the left to the word on the right that matches it.

Peace	German
Salaam	Chinese
Shalom	French
Meer	Korean
Irene	English
Ho Ping	Russian
Amani	Greek
Hey-wah	Spanish
Paix	Swahili
Paz	Japanese
Friede	Arabic
Pyung Wah	Hebrew

Here I Am, Lord

WORDS: Dan Schutte
MUSIC: Dan Schutte; adapt. by Carlton R. Young

night. _____ I will go Lord, _____ if you lead me. _____

_ I will hold your peo - ple in my heart.

Activities

1. Select a narrator to sing or speak the verses. Have remaining members sing the response contained in the refrain.

2. Read the story of Isaiah's vision found in Isaiah 6:1-8. Or, choose persons to read the following version according to the characters indicated:

Isaiah's Vision

Narrator 1: A long time ago during Bible times, there was a man named Isaiah. He was a prophet from Jerusalem. He told things to the kings that no one else could tell. There was a time when Isaiah had a startling vision. This is what happened.

Isaiah: I saw God, sitting way up high on a throne. God had on a royal robe that filled the temple. God was surrounded by angels. God's brightness was so great that the angels had to cover themselves as they flew about. I heard them saying over and over to one another: "Holy, holy, holy is the God of hosts; the whole earth is full of God's glory!"

Then I heard God's voice, and as God spoke, I felt the whole building shudder and shake. I could see billowing smoke filling up the whole place. Being in God's glorious presence was wonderful and terrifying all rolled into one. I felt God's goodness. I didn't feel deserving of what was happening to me. I found myself feeling guilty and sad for my wrongs and for being part of a disgraceful nation. I called out:

"I have seen God with my own eyes! What will become of me now?"

Narrator 2: Then one of the angels flew to Isaiah. The angel took some tongs and picked up a burning coal from the altar and touched Isaiah's lips with it. The angel said, "Isaiah, you don't have to feel guilty and sad anymore. You are forgiven for your wrongs." Then God spoke to Isaiah:

God: "Whom shall I send? Who will be my messenger?"

Narrator 1: And Isaiah answered:

Isaiah: "Here I am! Send me!"

Narrator 2: God wanted Isaiah to take God's message to the people. Isaiah agreed to be God's messenger. God warned him that being a messenger would not be easy—that there would be people who would not listen. But Isaiah still became God's messenger.[2]

3. Create paper bag puppets and dramatize the Bible story.

4. Invite discussion by asking: "What instances can you describe when you were less than kind to someone? What instance can you describe when whole groups of people were treated badly or unfairly? In what ways may people say they are sorry? Whom does God ask today to be God's messengers?"

This Little Light of Mine

2. Everywhere I go
3. All through the night

WORDS: Afro-American spiritual (Mt. 5:14-16)
MUSIC: Afro-American spiritual; adapt. by William Farley Smith

Activities

1. Sing the song with hand clapping.

2. Read Mark 4:21-23 and Luke 8:16. Call attention to the light as the gifts or talents God gives people to use for good in community. Ask group members to name some of these gifts or talents.

3. Have group members explore their gifts or talents. Have younger groups draw pictures of something they do very well that helps someone. Have older groups tape or pin a sheet of paper entitled "Gifts" on each member's back. Ask each member to write the gifts or talents they have observed on the papers of three of their group mates. When finished, have each person read the list and respond with: "Thank you for sharing," or "I appreciate your seeing that in me," or "I wasn't aware of it, but now I'll think about it." Put the papers on a bulletin board entitled "Our Gifts for God in Community." Adults may also find a personal inventory method to be helpful in exploring their spiritual gifts.[3]

4. Sing the song again with rhythm instruments and descant as indicated below.

5. Compare the message of this song with the message of the following song, "May God's Love Shine in Me."

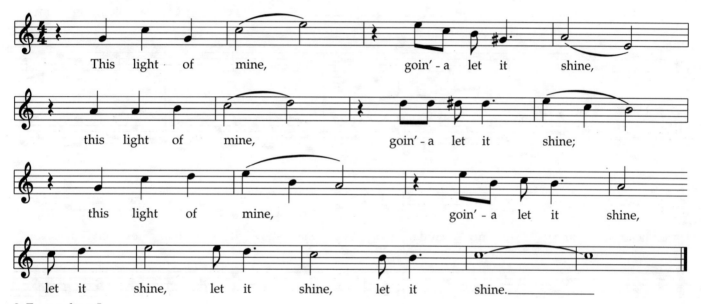

This light of mine, goin'-a let it shine, this light of mine, goin'-a let it shine; this light of mine, goin'-a let it shine, let it shine, let it shine, let it shine._____

2. Everywhere I go
3. All through the night

WORDS: Afro-American spiritual (Mt. 5:14-16)
MUSIC: Anne Wimberly

Descant © 1996 Abingdon Press

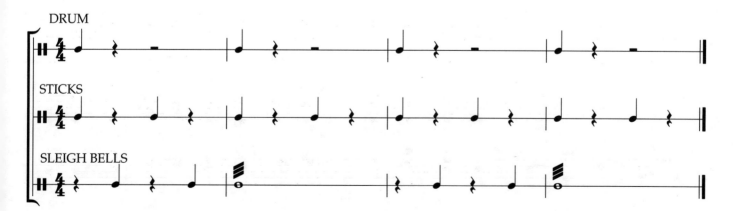

May God's Love Shine in Me

WORDS and MUSIC: Anne Streaty Wimberly
© 1996 Abingdon Press

A bear-er of kind-ness all a - round; _____ A mes - sen-ger as -

sur - ing love's in - crease _____ so true bro - ther-hood and sis - ter-hood a -

rit.   *a tempo*

bound. _____ Ev - ery-where I go, and in ev - ery-thing I

rit.   *a tempo*

do,   may God's   love   shine   in   me. _____

3. SING SONGS FROM MANY CULTURES

An Example

Mr. L leads the youth group. He discovered that some members of the class had been enrolled in foreign language classes or English as a second language. He thought about the lack of attention the youth group had paid to culture and language differences. He and the group decided together to spend some time learning about the ethnic cultural groups represented in their schools and to find songs to sing that tell about the Christian journeys of people in these groups.

The group invited speakers from various ethnic cultural groups to discuss their cultural and religious customs. Because their cross-cultural experiences began eight weeks before Christmas, they planned a culminating "festival" in which they met with youth and their pastors/leaders from local churches to develop a cross-cultural Christmas celebration.

The festival included a covered dish supper in which the youth and their families brought favorite dishes from their cultures. The supper was followed by a cross-cultural worship experience. The Christmas story was read from the Bible in the various languages represented, and songs were sung from cultures around the world. The festival ended with a candlelight ceremony in which each person lit the candle they had been given from a large candle representing Jesus Christ. They formed a circle as they came forward to light their candles. When all the candles were lit and the circle was complete, a representative from each cultural group gave a Christmas greeting in their own language.

Know What It Means to Sing Songs from Many Cultures

In our country, over thirty million people come from homes where English is not the first language. Most of these people are from Spanish-speaking backgrounds. However, this number also includes people from Asian and Pacific island cultures as well as people of German, Italian, and Eastern European heritages. There is a growing awareness in the church of the variations in Christian music among the world's people, and Christians are becoming increasingly sensitive to language differences.

Harold Best reminds us that we should cherish this diversity because God does. God imagines and creates with endless variety and calls it good. God also gives to people the creativity and the wisdom to fashion songs that convey the wholeness of praise and worship to God. And, most important, no one culture can convey it all.[1] Best describes the world of musical creativity as a "musical pentecost" and encourages us to seek out and welcome in our own lives the variety of music inherent in it.[2] In doing so, we discover God's Spirit throughout the diverse Body of Christ—the same Spirit that makes us one.

When we welcome the varieties of music of God's people as part of what we do in our church groups, we show our awareness of the musical pentecost. In doing so, we foster cultural sensitivity and appreciation.[3] We open the way for exploring historical realities that form a basis for people's expressions of the faith. We allow our own lives to be enriched. What songs may we choose? There are *culture-referenced songs* and *language-specific songs* appearing in songbooks. Culture-referenced songs contain musical material, folk and composed, originating in a specific ethnic cultural group within this country and around the world. In these songs, the English language is used. The native language of the ethnic cultural group, if different from English, does not appear. Culture-referenced songs also include music from the African American heritage and folk music created in Anglo-American culture, both of which employ the English language. Songs from the African American heritage sometimes appear with a language dialect. In songbooks, references to the cultural origin of these songs typically appear on the same page as the songs.

Language-specific songs are ethnic cultural songs, folk and composed, from within this country and around the world, that include ethnic cultural melodies and native language. The language is specific to the ethnic cultural context out of which the songs come. In songbooks designed for predominantly English-speaking people, the ethnic cultural language is typically presented with phonetic spellings, called transliterations. The transliterations are usually followed by English translations. Some songs, particularly favorite hymns originally written in English, include other language translations often using phonetic spellings. In what follows, we will look at several culture-referenced and language-specific songs.

How to Make It Happen

Examples of culture-referenced and language-specific songs appear on the following pages with suggestions for their use. A separate section of culture-referenced and language-specific Christmas and Easter songs are included. Some general guidelines include the following:

- Make a special point to include culture-referenced and language-specific songs as part of a group's ongoing musical involvement. Seek out persons from ethnic cultural groups, group members or others within the church who are proficient in a particular language, or language teachers from local schools to help with word pronunciations.
- Use culture-referenced songs and language-specific songs to experience and talk about creative and gifted ways God's people throughout the world express their faith.
- Use culture-referenced songs and language-specific songs as part of units on God's people within the local church, community, nation, and the world.[4] Use them as part of missions studies also.
- Include culture-referenced songs and language-specific songs as integral parts of worship experiences. Open and close worship with these songs. Recite the words, using both English and phonetic spellings, before entering prayer. Use songs that address God directly as prayers. Include words of songs, both English and phonetic spellings, as parts of litanies and as responses to sentence prayers.
- Celebrate the seasons of the church year with culture-referenced songs and language-specific songs. Organize a Christmas or Easter festival, for example, using the songs included in the special section in this chapter.
- Add rhythm instruments as accompaniments to songs, where indicated.
- Create movement or dance to depict the song messages. Use colored streamers, scarves, and balloons in this creative activity.
- Add a descant where it appears with a song.
- Seek out information about the cultural group from which the songs come. Explore historical materials that describe various cultural contexts and customs and the journeys of cultural groups in this country. Examples of materials appear in the Resource List at the end of this book.
- Look for additional songs from many cultures to sing and to engage in creative activities.
- Use the activities listed under each song.

Let Us Sing to Christ Today

WORDS: Tom Colvin
MUSIC: Gonja folk song; adapt. by Tom Colvin

Activities

1. Call attention to the origin of the song in Ghana, Africa.

2. For discussion ask: "What are some reasons for singing to, praying to, trusting in, learning from, working for, walking with, and living in Christ? In what ways do we feel welcomed as part of our church? In what ways may we welcome others in our church and community?"

3. Have the group draw a "welcome mural" on a long sheet of newsprint showing brothers, sisters, neighbors, wise ones, workers, children, and Christians who make up their community and church. Include on the mural names of the people, if they are known. Look up ways of saying "welcome" in different languages and include them on the mural. When the mural is complete, have group members name the people they drew and why they included them on the welcome mural.

4. Sing the song with drum beat.

May the Lord, Mighty God

WORDS: Adapted from scripture
MUSIC: Chinese folk tune; attr. Pao-chen Li

Activities

1. Call attention to the Chinese origin of this song.

2. Let the entire group sing the melody of the song together. Then have all group members learn the Voice II part. After the group can comfortably sing both parts, have half the group sing the Voice II part.

3. Invite the group to join hands in a circle, and sing the song as a closing benediction.

Many and Great, O God

Accompany with a steady drumbeat - ♩ ♩ ♩

WORDS: Joseph R. Renville; paraphrased by Philip Frazier
MUSIC: Traditional Dakota melody

Activities

1. Call attention to the Native American origin of the melody.

2. For discussion ask: "How do the earth, sky, stars, mountains, plains, and water bring us to greater awareness of our relationship and the relationship of all things to God? What are some of the gifts God has given you that make you a fully alive person? What does eternal life mean to you? Are there ways in which we as Christians prepare to receive eternal life?"

3. Sing with drum beat and rattles. Have one or two group members pantomime.

Kum Ba Yah
(Come By Here)

2. Someone's praying, Lord.
3. Someone's crying, Lord.
4. Someone needs you, Lord.

5. Someone's singing, Lord.
6. Let us praise the Lord.

SMALL DRUM

WORDS: Afro-American spiritual
MUSIC: Afro-American spiritual; harm. by Carlton R. Young
Harm. © 1989 The United Methodist Publishing House

Activities

1. Call attention to the African American origin of this song and the African dialect words "Kum ba yah," which mean "come by here."

2. For discussion ask: "Who is the Lord? What are various names we use to address God?"

3. Have the group create additional verses to the song.

4. Have the group add hand motions appropriate to the verses of the song.

Bless the Lord, O My Soul

Bless the Lord, O _____ my soul; And all that is with-in me, bless God's ho - ly name!

Bless the Lord, O _____ my soul. And for - get not all God's ben - e - fits.

WORDS: Adapted from scripture
MUSIC: Appalachian folk melody

Activities

1. Call attention to the origin of the song melody in Appalachia in early American times.

2. For discussion ask: "What does it mean to bless God? Why is it important to bless God? What are various ways we can bless God?

How do the words of the song compare with the words of Psalm 103:1-2?" Recite the scripture reference and the scripture passage. Then sing the song as a group.

3. Divide the group in half with one half singing the sections of the song designated for the leader and the other half singing the sections of the song designated for response.

Dear Lord, Lead Me Day by Day

1. Dear Lord, lead me day by day; make me stead-fast, wise and strong;
2. Dear Lord, lead me day by day; make me fol-low and o-bey
3. Now with con-fi-dence I sing joy-ous prais-es to our God,

hap-py most of all to know that my dear Lord loves me so.
faith-ful-ly your words of life, that your love ev-er a-bide.
and with up-right heart I give ten-der care and sym-pa-thy.

Refrain

Praise to God, fount of love, praise from morn till the set of sun;

praise at home, praise in church; praise to God ev-ery-where on earth.

WORDS: Francisca Asuncion
MUSIC: Philippine folk melody; arr by Francisca Asuncion
© 1983 The United Methodist Publishing House

Activities

1. Call attention to the Philippine origin of this song.

2. For discussion ask: "Why do we need God to lead us every day? How do we become aware of God's direction in our lives? What may prevent us from discovering and heeding God's direction?"

3. Instead of singing verses 1 and 2, speak them as a prayer. Create additional verses to be included in the prayer. End with "Amen" instead of singing the refrain.

4. Sing the refrain with drum accompaniment or hand claps. Add the descant shown below:

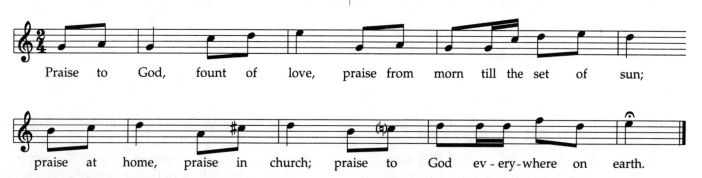

Praise to God, fount of love, praise from morn till the set of sun;

praise at home, praise in church; praise to God ev-ery-where on earth.

MUSIC: Anne Wimberly
© 1996 Abingdon Press

Daw-Kee, Aim Daw-Tsi-Taw
(Great Spirit, Now I Pray)

WORDS: Kiowa prayer; para. by Libby Littlechief
MUSIC: Native American melody; arr. by Charles Boynton

Activities

1. Call attention to this prayer from the Kiowa tribe of Native Americans from the Great Plains.

2. For discussion ask: "Who is the Great Spirit? How do you address God when you pray? Why do you pray? What are some special times when you pray?"

3. Sing the prayer with quiet drum beat and rattles.

4. Use the song as an opening to short sentence prayers by individual group members focused on specific concerns. Follow each sentence prayer with the song as a response.

Pues Si Vivimos
(When We Are Living)

1. Pues si vi - vi - mos _____ pa - ra Él vi - vi - mos _____
2. En es - ta vi - da, _____ fru - tos he - mos de dar _____
3. En la tris - te - za _____ y en el do - lor, _____
4. En es - te mun - do, _____ he - mos de en - con - trar _____

1. When we are liv - ing, _____ it is in Christ Je - sus, _____
2. Through all our liv - ing, _____ we our fruits must give. _____
3. Mid times of sor - row _____ and in times of pain, _____
4. A - cross this wide world, _____ we shall al - ways find _____

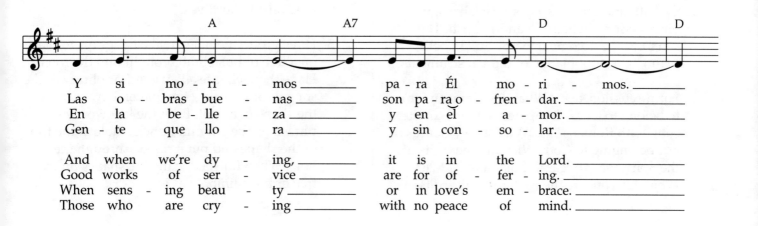

Y si mo - ri - mos _____ pa - ra Él mo - ri - mos.
Las o - bras bue - nas _____ son pa - ra o - fren - dar. _____
En la be - lle - za _____ y en el a - mor. _____
Gen - te que llo - ra _____ y sin con - so - lar. _____

And when we're dy - ing, _____ it is in the Lord. _____
Good works of ser - vice _____ are for of - fer - ing. _____
When sens - ing beau - ty _____ or in love's em - brace. _____
Those who are cry - ing _____ with no peace of mind. _____

WORDS: St. 1 anon., trans. by Elise S. Eslinger; sts. 2-4 Roberto Escamilla, trans. by George Lockwood (Romans 14:8)
MUSIC: Traditional Spanish melody

Trans. © 1989 The United Methodist Publishing House

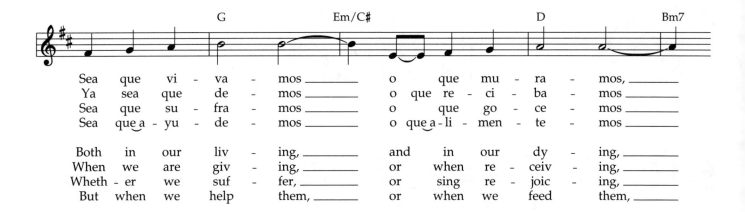

					G				Em/C♯						D				Bm7	

Sea que vi - va - mos _____ o que mu - ra - mos, _____
Ya sea que de - mos _____ o que re - ci - ba - mos _____
Sea que su - fra - mos _____ o que go - ce - mos _____
Sea que a - yu - de - mos _____ o que a - li - men - te - mos _____

Both in our liv - ing, _____ and in our dy - ing, _____
When we are giv - ing, _____ or when re - ceiv - ing, _____
Wheth - er we suf - fer, _____ or sing re - joic - ing, _____
But when we help them, _____ or when we feed them, _____

Refrain

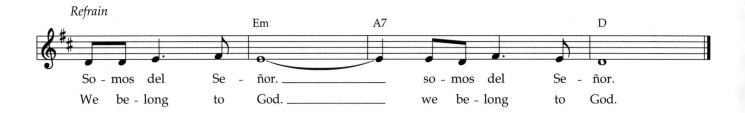

			Em		A7				D	

So - mos del Se - ñor. _____ so - mos del Se - ñor.
We be - long to God. _____ we be - long to God.

Activities

1. Call attention to the song's Spanish origin. Sing the song in Spanish and English. The song may be accompanied by guitar, bells, piano, or a combination of these instruments.

2. For discussion, ask: "What does it mean for us to belong to God? Compare the words of the song with Romans 14:8. What are evidences of our belonging to God? What are the fruits of the Spirit that appear in Galatians 4:22-26? What, for you, are the most difficult fruits of the Spirit to maintain? Why? How is it possible for us to do our best to show the fruits of the Spirit in our lives?"

3. Have group members make hang-ups to place on a tree or bush limb brought into the room. Have them choose a key word or phrase in the song. From construction paper, have each cut the shape of a fruit. Print the key word or phrase on the cut-out. Punch a hole at the top of the shape and put a ribbon through the hole. When finished, hang the shapes on the tree or bush limb.

Heleluyan
(Alleluia)

He - le - lu - yan, he - le - lu - yan; he - le, he - le - lu - yan;

he - le - lu - yan, he - le - lu - yan; he - le, he - le - lu - yan.

WORDS: Traditional Muscogee (Creek) Indian
MUSIC: Traditional Muscogee (Creek) Indian; transcription by Charles H. Webb

Activities

1. Call attention to the song's origin in the Muscogee tribe of Native Americans.

2. Have group members sing the song in a circle, holding their neighbor's hands. Have them raise their clasped hands above their heads and sway their arms rhythmically to a drum beat.

3. For discussion, ask: "What are some of the things that have happened to you that made you want to say 'Hallelujah!'?"

4. Sing "Heleluyan" before and after reading Psalms 146–150.

5. Read the story about "The Rejoicing in Heaven" found in Revelation 19:1-8. Sing the song in place of the word "Hallelujah!" where it appears in the story.

Jesus Loves Me

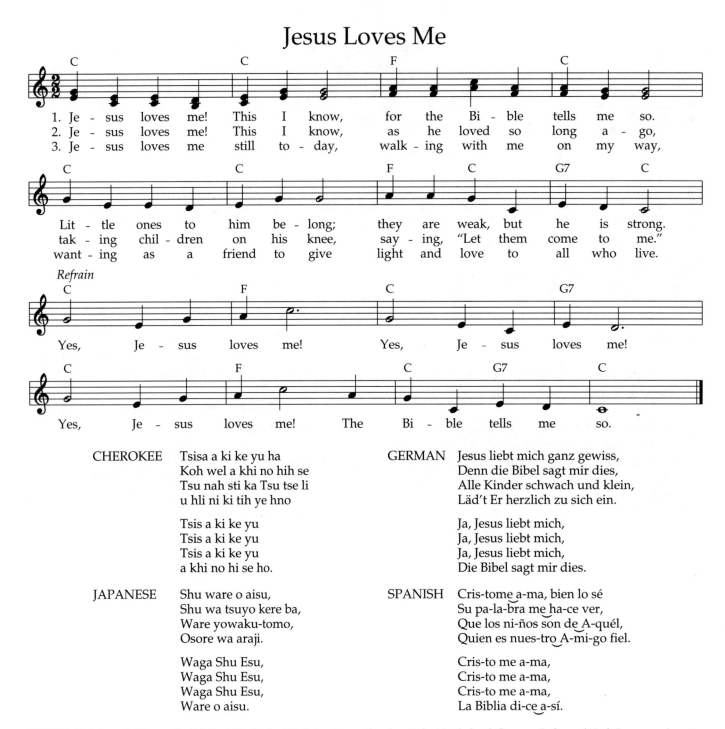

1. Je - sus loves me! This I know, for the Bi - ble tells me so.
2. Je - sus loves me! This I know, as he loved so long a - go,
3. Je - sus loves me still to - day, walk - ing with me on my way,

Lit - tle ones to him be - long; they are weak, but he is strong.
tak - ing chil - dren on his knee, say - ing, "Let them come to me."
want - ing as a friend to give light and love to all who live.

Refrain

Yes, Je - sus loves me! Yes, Je - sus loves me!

Yes, Je - sus loves me! The Bi - ble tells me so.

CHEROKEE	Tsisa a ki ke yu ha	GERMAN	Jesus liebt mich ganz gewiss,
	Koh wel a khi no hih se		Denn die Bibel sagt mir dies,
	Tsu nah sti ka Tsu tse li		Alle Kinder schwach und klein,
	u hli ni ki tih ye hno		Läd't Er herzlich zu sich ein.
	Tsis a ki ke yu		Ja, Jesus liebt mich,
	Tsis a ki ke yu		Ja, Jesus liebt mich,
	Tsis a ki ke yu		Ja, Jesus liebt mich,
	a khi no hi se ho.		Die Bibel sagt mir dies.
JAPANESE	Shu ware o aisu,	SPANISH	Cris-tome a-ma, bien lo sé
	Shu wa tsuyo kere ba,		Su pa-la-bra me ha-ce ver,
	Ware yowaku-tomo,		Que los ni-ños son de A-quél,
	Osore wa araji.		Quien es nues-tro A-mi-go fiel.
	Waga Shu Esu,		Cris-to me a-ma,
	Waga Shu Esu,		Cris-to me a-ma,
	Waga Shu Esu,		Cris-to me a-ma,
	Ware o aisu.		La Biblia di-ce a-sí.

WORDS: St. 1 Anna B. Warner; Sts. 2-3 David Rutherford McGuire; trans.: Cherokee, Robert Bushyhead; German, *Psalter und Harfe;* Japanese, phonetic transcription, Mas Kawashima; Spanish, *Himnario Metodista.*
MUSIC: William B. Bradbury

Activities

1. Call attention to the meaning of the song for people of all races and ethnic cultural groups.

2. Read the scriptures, Mark 10:13-16, Matthew 19:13-15, and Luke 18:15-17. For discussion, ask: "What is the best part of being a child? What is difficult? Why? How may grown-ups help children experience God's love?"

3. Have group members draw pictures of children gathered around Jesus. Ask them to include themselves in the picture.

Amazing Grace

1. A - maz - ing grace! how sweet the sound that
2. 'Twas grace that taught my heart to fear, and
3. Through man - y dan - gers, toils, and snares, I
4. The Lord has prom - ised good to me, his
5. Yea, when this flesh and heart shall fail, and
6. When we've been there ten thou - sand years, bright

saved a wretch like me! I once was lost, but
grace my fears re - lieved; how pre - cious did that
have al - read - y come; 'tis grace hath brought me
word my hope se - cures; he will my shield and
mor - tal life shall cease, I shall pos - sess, with -
shin - ing as the sun, we've no less days to

now am found; was blind, but now I see.
grace ap - pear the hour I first be - lieved.
safe thus far, and grace will lead me home.
por - tion be, as long as life en - dures.
in the veil, a life of joy and peace.
sing God's praise than when we'd first be - gun.

CHEROKEE

Ooh nay thla nah, hee oo way gee.
E gah gwoo yah hay ee.
Naw gwoo joe sah, we you low say,
E gah gwoo yah ho nah.

NAVAJO

Nizhónígo jooba' ditts' a'
Yisdáshíítínígíí,
Lah yóóííyá, k'ad shénáhoosdzin,
Doo eesh'íí da ńt'éé.

KIOWA

Daw k'ee da ha dawtsahy he tsow'haw
Daw k'ee da ha dawtsahy hee.
Bay dawtsahy taw, gaw aym ow thah t'aw,
Daw k'ee da ha dawtsahy h'ee.

CREEK

Po ya fek cha he thlat ah tet
Ah non ah cha pa kas
Cha fee kee o funnan la kus
Um e ha ta la yus.

CHOCTAW

Shilombish holitopa ma!
Ishmminti pulla cha
Hatak ilbusha pia ha
Is pi yukpalashke.

WORDS: John Newton; st. 6 anon.; phonetic transcription Cherokee, Kiowa, Creek, Choctaw as sung in Oklahoma Indian Missionary Conference;
    Navajo phonetic transcription, Albert Tsosi (1 Chr. 17:16-17)
MUSIC: 19th cent. USA melody; harm. by Edwin O. Excell

Activities

1. Call attention to the many different Native American nations and languages in our country.

2. Also call attention to the popularity of this hymn across cultures and generations. Discuss reasons for this.

3. Add the descant below.

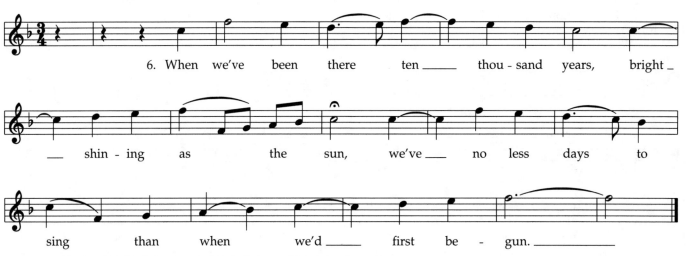

DESCANT: Charles H. Webb; from *The United Methodist Hymnal, Music Supplement II*
© 1993 Abingdon Press

SING CHRISTMAS SONGS FROM MANY CULTURES

Read: Luke 2:1-7
Sing the song, using different small groups in each verse, and accompanied by drum.

That Boy-Child of Mary

Refrain

That boy-child of Mary was born in a stable, a manger his cradle in Bethlehem.

Fine

1. What shall we call him, child of the manger? What name is given in Bethlehem?
2. His name is Jesus, God ever-with us, God given for us in Bethlehem.
3. How can he save us, how can he help us, born here among us in Bethlehem.
4. Gift of the Father, to human mother, makes him our brother of Bethlehem.
5. One with the Father, he is our Savior, heaven-sent helper of Bethlehem.
6. Gladly we praise him, love and adore him, give ourselves to him of Bethlehem.

D.C.

WORDS: Tom Colvin (Lk. 2:7)
MUSIC: Trad. Malawi melody; adapt. by Tom Colvin

Read: Luke 2:8-14
Sing the song as a whole group. Then sing it as a round.

Gloria, Gloria

Glo - ri - a, glo - ri - a, in ex - cel - sis De - o!

Glo - ri - a, glo - ri - a! Al - le - lu - ia! Al - le - lu - ia!

May be sung as a canon.

WORDS: Luke 2:14
MUSIC: Jacques Berthier and the Community of Taizé

Music © 1979 Les Presses de Taizé by permission of G.I.A. Publications, Inc.

Sing this refrain, using drum accompaniment.

Go, Tell It on the Mountain

Go, tell it on the moun - tain, o - ver the hills and ev - ery - where;

go, tell it on the moun - tain, that Je - sus Christ is born.

WORDS: John W. Work, Jr.
MUSIC: Afro-American spiritual; adapt. and arr. by William Farley Smith.

Adapt. and arr. © 1989 The United Methodist Publishing House

Read: Luke 2:15-16

Sing the song as a group. Then divide into two groups and sing the two parts of the canon (like a round).

Noël, Noël

Canon

Spiritedly

No - ël, No - ël, The shep-herds leave the vil - lage, No -

No - ël, No - ël, The shep-herds leave the

ël, No - ël, They leave their sleep - ing flocks, To

vil - lage, No - ël, No - ël, They leave their sleep - ing

seek the child; They find him in a hum - ble sta - ble,

flocks, To seek the child; They find him in a

Oh! No - ël! No - ël! The earth is filled with joy! No - ël!

hum - ble sta - ble, Oh! No - ël! The earth is filled with joy! No - ël!

WORDS and MUSIC: Old French carol

49

Read: Luke 2:20
Sing the song and add the drum part as shown.

African Noel

WORDS AND MUSIC: Liberian folk song

SING EASTER SONGS FROM MANY CULTURES

Read: Mark 11:1-10
Sing the song in Spanish and English.

Mantos y Palmas
(Filled with Excitement)

WORDS: Rubén Ruiz Avila; trans. by Gertrude C. Suppe (Mt. 21: 8-9; Mk. 11:8-10; Lk. 19:36-38; Jn. 12:12-13)
MUSIC: Rubén Ruiz Avila; arr. by Alvin Schutmaat

Read: Mark 14:55-65; 15:1-15

Sing the song, beginning with the whole group on verse 1, followed by small groups on each of the remaining verses. End with the whole group humming the entire tune.

Were You There

1. Were you there when they cru-ci-fied my Lord?
2. Were you there when they nailed him to the tree?
3. Were you there when they laid him in the tomb?

Were you there when they cru-ci-fied my Lord?
Were you there when they nailed him to the tree?
Were you there when they laid him in the tomb?

Refrain

Oh _____ some-times it

caus-es me to trem-ble, trem-ble, trem-ble. _____

Were you there when they cru-ci-fied my Lord?
Were you there when they nailed him to the tree?
Were you there when they laid him in the tomb?

Chords have been simplified for classroom use.

WORDS: Afro-American spiritual
MUSIC: Afro-American spiritual; adapt. and arr. by William Farley Smith

Adapt. and arr. © 1989 The United Methodist Publishing House

Read: Matthew 28:1-6
Sing the song with parts.

Jesus Christ Is Risen Today

WORDS: St. 1-3 *Lyra Davidica*; St. 4 Charles Wesley
MUSIC: *Lyra Davidica;* adapt. from *The Compleat Psalmodist*

4. TELL BIBLE STORIES THROUGH SONG

An Example

*M*s. M's children look forward to the stories they are going to hear from the Bible and the songs they sing about those stories. They routinely burst into the room, bubbling with questions: "What story are you going to tell us today? I'll bet it's a Bible story. Are you going to tell that story about Zach. . . what's his name again? I like that story! Can we sing the song that tells about Zach's story? Can we sing the song about Daniel? It's neat!"

Know What It Means to Tell Bible Stories Through Song

Over the years, people have used music to communicate Bible stories and sayings that held great meaning for them. Through the songs they wrote, they tell of the trials and triumphs of people during Old Testament times with whom they identified. We have already discovered that songwriters retell the psalmists' words in their own musical idioms. Songwriters also put into musical form the New Testament stories of Jesus. As we saw in the preceding chapter, songs tell of Jesus' birth, death, and resurrection. But songs also present sayings of Jesus and messages about the Christian life told by apostles in the early Christian church. Scripture songs have become voices of the storytellers who wrote them and testimonies of people who were touched by God's story as revealed in the Bible. When we sing them, we learn in a new and creative way the message of the gospel. We become storytellers of the gospel.

Through our use of songs that relate Bible stories and sayings, we creatively connect our groups with God's story as found in scripture. We draw their attention to the unfolding drama of God's story and to the importance of their study of it and participation in it. We highlight the influence of scripture on the lives of the people who wrote the songs and on our lives as well. We stimulate in groups their potential for creative responses to scripture and to the songs they sing. We make evident the pivotal role of scripture in our lives as Christians.

How to Make It Happen

Selected songs that relate Old Testament and New Testament Bible stories and sayings appear on upcoming pages along with the scripture passages on which they are based. When we present Bible story or scripture songs, we may do the following:

- Begin or end Bible study with the musical version of the story, or insert music throughout the study.
- Ask group members to find the story or text in the Bible and/or to remember the book of the Bible from which it comes.
- Read in the Bible the passage to which the song refers. Discuss ways in which the Bible story/text appearing in the song is similar to or different from how it appears in the Bible. Discuss why this might be so.
- Invite group members to recall key actors, settings, events, actions, words, outcomes, and meanings found in the Bible story. If the song communicates a scripture saying, have group members identify key words, meanings, and who communicated them. Discuss why they were said.
- Have group members role-play the Bible story or use puppets to tell the story. Use the music, played on the piano, taped, or hummed, as a theme song for the role play or puppet drama. Create pictures, murals, hand puppets, clay figures, and other art work that summarize the Bible story/text. Taped recordings of the songs may be played as group members create art work.
- Invite group members to present their art work and tell what it means as well as why they chose to do what they did. The group may sing the songs after they present their art work.
- Arrange art work in the order of the story progression. Videotape the art work as selected group members serve as narrators. Have remaining group members sing the Bible story or scripture saying at the beginning and end of the video, or play an audiotape of the group singing the music throughout the videotaping process.
- Review Bible stories and songs previously done for enjoyment and to reinforce their meanings. Explore with groups how the stories/sayings apply to their everyday lives.

AN INVITATION TO STORYTELLING

Beneath the Storytelling Tree

* Woodblock enters here and continues through refrain only.

WORDS and MUSIC: James Ritchie
ARRANGEMENT: Timothy Edmonds

Scripture: Genesis 1:1-5

God Made the Earth

Optional Handbells or Glockenspiel

WORDS and MUSIC: Susan Eltringham (based on Genesis 1:10)
© 1993 Abingdon Press

Scripture: Daniel 6:10-28; Jonah 2:1-10; Daniel 3:19-30

Didn't My Lord Deliver Daniel

Did-n't my Lord de-liv-er Dan - iel, de-li-ver Dan - iel, de-liv-er Dan - iel?

Did-n't my Lord de-liv-er Dan - iel, And why not - a ev-e-ry - one?

1. He de-liv-er'd Dan-iel from the li-on's den, Jo-nah from the bel-ly of the

whale, and the He-brew chil-dren from the fie - ry fur-nace, And why not ev-e-ry - one?

2. The moon run down in a pur-ple stream, The sun for-bear to shine, And

ev - e - ry star dis-ap - pear, King Je - sus shall be mine.

3. The wind blows east, and the wind blows west, It blows like the judg-ment day,

And ev-ery poor soul that nev-er did pray, 'll be glad to pray that day.

4. I set my foot on the Gos-pel ship, And the ship it be-gin to sail,

It land-ed me o - ver on Ca-naan's shore, And I'll nev-er come back an-y more.

WORDS and MUSIC: Traditional

Go Down, Moses

3. No more shall they in bondage toil, ...
   Let them come out with Egypt's spoil, ...

4. When Israel out of Egypt came, ...
   And left the proud oppressive land, ...

5. O, 'twas a dark and dismal night, ...
   When Moses led the Israelites, ...

6. 'Twas good old Moses and Aaron, too, ...
   'Twas they that led the armies through, ...

7. The Lord told Moses what to do, ...
   To lead the children of Israel through, ...

8. O come along, Moses, you'll not get lost, ...
   Stretch out your rod and come across, ...

9. As Israel stood by the water side, ...
   At the command of God it did divide, ...

10. When they had reached the other shore, ...
    They sang the song of triumph o'er, ...

11. Pharaoh said he would go across, ...
    But Pharaoh and his host were lost, ...

12. Oh, Moses, the cloud shall clear the way, ...
    A fire by night, a shade by day, ...

WORDS and MUSIC: Traditional

Joshua Fit de Battle of Jericho

WORDS and MUSIC: Traditional

Little David, Play on Your Harp

1. Lit-tle Da - vid was a shep-herd boy, He killed Go - li - ath and shout-ed for joy.
2. ____ Josh-u - a was the son of Nun, He nev - er would quit till the work was done.
3. Done told you once, done told you twice, There's sin-ners in hell for shoot - ing dice.

WORDS and MUSIC: Traditional

Scripture: Psalm 137
Sing the song in unison and then as a round.

By the Waters of Babylon

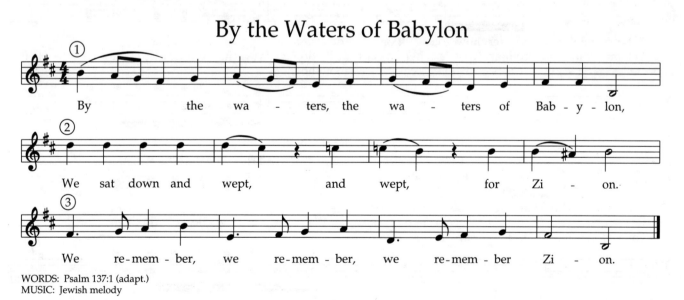

WORDS: Psalm 137:1 (adapt.)
MUSIC: Jewish melody

Ezek'el Saw de Wheel

With spirit

E-ze-k'el saw de wheel 'Way up in de mid-dle o' de air, E-ze-k'el saw de wheel 'Way in de mid-dle o' de air. De big wheel run by faith, De lit-tle wheel run by de Grace o' God, A wheel in a wheel 'Way in de mid-dle o' de air.

Fine

LEADER

1. Bet-ter min', my sis-ter, how you walk on de cross,
2. Let me tell you, broth-er, what a hyp-o-crite will do,
3. Ol' Sa-tan wears a club - foot shoe,

RESPONSE

'Way in de mid-dle o' de air,

LEADER

Yo'
He'll
If

RESPONSE

foot might slip an yo soul be los'.
low-rate you an' he'll low-rate me.
you don' min', he'll slip it on you.

'Way in de mid-dle o' de air.

D.C.

WORDS: Traditional
MUSIC: Traditional; harm. by J. Jefferson Cleveland

SONGS THAT TELL NEW TESTAMENT STORIES

Scripture: Mark 1:16-20; Matthew 4:18-22;
Luke 5:1-11

Disciple Rap

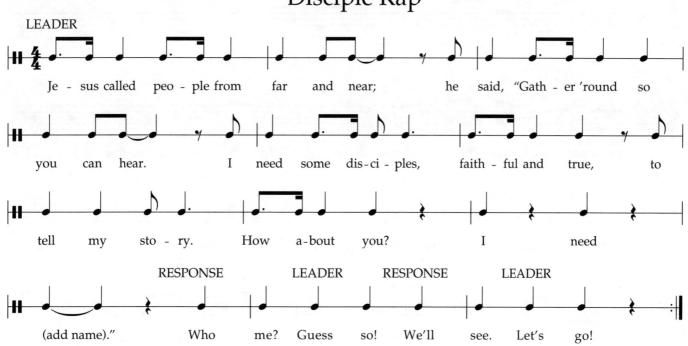

Je-sus called peo-ple from far and near; he said, "Gath-er 'round so
you can hear. I need some dis-ci-ples, faith-ful and true, to
tell my sto-ry. How a-bout you? I need

RESPONSE   LEADER   RESPONSE   LEADER

(add name)." Who me? Guess so! We'll see. Let's go!

WORDS and MUSIC: Susan Isbell and James Ritchie
© 1990 by Graded Press

Scripture: Mark 12:30-31; Matthew 22:36-40;
Luke 10:25-28

This Is My Commandment

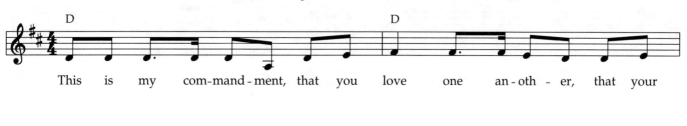

This is my com-mand-ment, that you love one an-oth-er, that your

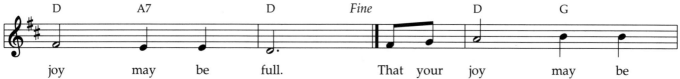

joy may be full. That your joy may be

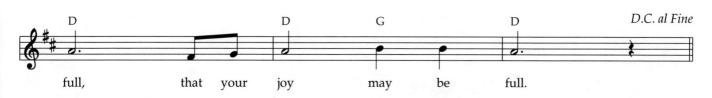

full, that your joy may be full.

WORDS: John 15:11-12
MUSIC: Anonymous
Music arrangement © 1983 Graded Press

Come Down, Zacchaeus [1]

Come down from the syc-a-more tree, Zac-chae-us, come down from the

syc-a-more tree; Zac-chae-us come down from the syc-a-more tree, for sal-

va-tion is come un-to thee. To-day is sal-

va-tion day; to-mor-row may nev-er come.

Je-sus is call-ing you now to come down from the syc-a-more

1. tree! Zac-chae-us, To- 2. tree! Zac-chae-us, come down.

WORDS and MUSIC: Ghana folk song; translated by Dorothy Akota; transcribed by Anne Wimberly
© 1996 Abingdon Press

The Golden Rule

WORDS: Luke 6:31 (adapted)
MUSIC: Anne Streaty Wimberly

The Jailhouse Rocked

Spirited

1. Paul and Si - las were put in jail, put in jail,
2. Paul and Si - las sang and prayed, sang and prayed,
3. Paul and Si - las felt a shake, felt a shake,
4. Then the jail - er did a - wake, did a - wake,

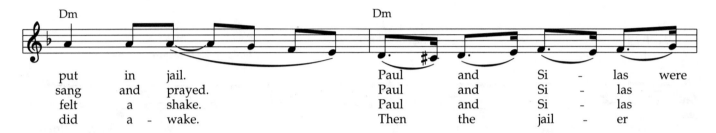

put in jail.   Paul and Si - las were
sang and prayed.   Paul and Si - las
felt a shake.   Paul and Si - las
did a - wake.   Then the jail - er

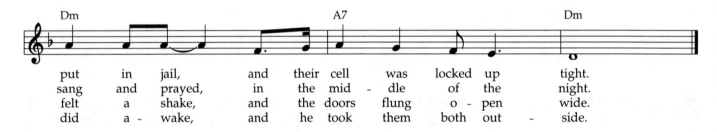

put in jail, and their cell was locked up tight.
sang and prayed, in the mid - dle of the night.
felt a shake, and the doors flung o - pen wide.
did a - wake, and he took them both out - side.

5. Next the jailer asked of them, asked of them, asked of them.
Next the jailer asked of them, just how can I be saved?

6. Paul and Silas answered him, answered him, answered him.
Paul and Silas answered him, "Believe in Jesus Christ."

7. So the jailer did a turnabout, turnabout, turnabout.
So the jailer did a turnabout, and the jailer's life was changed.

WORDS: Sue Downing
MUSIC: Traditional, "Joshua"

Words and music arrangement © 1994 by Cokesbury

Scripture: Revelation 3:20

Somebody's Knocking at Your Door

2. Can't you hear Him?
3. Answer Jesus.
4. Jesus calls you.
5. Can't you trust Him?

WORDS: Traditional (Afro-American spiritual)
MUSIC: Traditional (Afro-American spiritual); harm. by J. Jefferson Cleveland and Verolga Nix
Harm. © 1981 by Abingdon Press

5. TELL ABOUT CHURCH TRADITIONS THROUGH SONG

An Example

The first week of each month over a period of three months, the church school youth and adults met for thirty minutes after a shortened regular church school session to explore together several traditional aspects of the church's worship life. The assemblies resulted from a questionnaire given by the education committee on aspects of church tradition that people would like to know more about. The committee discovered that people wanted to know more about the origins and meanings of the confessions of faith they recite and the psalter they often sing during the worship service.

At the first assembly, they explored the origin and meanings of the Apostles' Creed. The second assembly focused on the Nicene Creed. The third assembly highlighted the psalter. At each assembly, they heard a short history of each topic. They discussed the words of the creeds and sang them. They discussed how the psalter is chosen for each Sunday. They discovered meanings of these acts of worship in which they had been involved but had not fully understood.

Know What It Means to Tell About Church Traditions in Song

Songs reveal traditions of the church that we carry out in Christian worship and life. The creeds and psalter are among these time-honored traditions. Songs chronicle the creeds of the church. They are part of the "call and response" pattern of reading and singing as we use the psalter in public worship.

When we include in church group experiences songs that reflect these church traditions, we raise awareness of the integral role of music in every aspect of the church's life. We not only draw attention to these church traditions, but we also create an opportunity to explore them and other traditions in order to enhance people's understanding.

In the sections below, we will focus on songs that communicate various aspects of our traditions. These include the Apostles' and Nicene Creeds, the Gloria Patri, the Doxology, the church calendar and the Psalter. Historical information and suggestions for using both these songs are included.

The Apostles' Creed

As a regular part of Sunday worship, we recite a version of the Apostles' Creed. When we recite the traditional version, we say:

I believe in God the Father Almighty,
    maker of heaven and earth;

And in Jesus Christ his only Son our Lord:
    who was conceived by the Holy Spirit,
        born of the Virgin Mary,
        suffered under Pontius Pilate,
        was crucified, dead, and buried;
the third day he rose from the dead;
he ascended into heaven,
    and sitteth at the right hand of God the Father
        Almighty;
from thence he shall come to judge the quick and
    the dead.

I believe in the Holy Spirit,
    the holy catholic church,
    the communion of saints,
    the forgiveness of sins,
    the resurrection of the body,
    and the life everlasting. Amen.

Where Did It Come From?

The Apostles' Creed is understood as a summary of the faith of the twelve apostles of Jesus Christ. It is the oldest expression of the truths of the faith we profess as Christians.

The Apostles' Creed was part of the rite of baptism in the early Christian community. Through the creed, the Christian vowed to forsake all others to be loyal only to God.[1] In the sixth century, it was used as preparation for communion. By the tenth century, people of the congregation customarily sang the creed, and eventually choirs took over singing it.[2] It has become the profession of faith of Christian churches throughout the world, and is regarded as the core of the Christian faith.[3]

How to Use the Song

The following song is a musical arrangement of the Apostles' Creed. The words paraphrase the traditional spoken version of the creed. When we present the song in a group, begin by giving the historical information provided above. We may ask groups to:

- Hold a "council meeting" to discuss the meaning of the Apostles' Creed for today. Complete the remaining suggested activities as part of the meeting.
- Recite the Apostles' Creed as it appears in the spoken version. Then read the paraphrased words in the song and learn to sing the song.
- Discuss ways the song text differs from the traditional spoken version. For this activity and the following ones, divide the group into small units of three or four people. Ask them to select a unit leader and reporter. Ask the reporter to record responses on newsprint or paper in readiness to report to the whole group.

- Explore meanings they assign to the traditional version and thoughts and feelings about the musical version.
- Consider why the creed continues to be used today.
- Explore the importance of the creed to how we live our everyday lives. Answer the questions: "What difference does it now make? What difference should it make?"
- Explore questions the Apostles' Creed raises for you. Consider also some answers to the questions or suggest ways to get answers to the questions.
- Using your own words, express what you believe.
- Receive the reports from each unit on their discussion of the above items. Recite the Apostles' Creed once again and sing the song again.

The Apostles' Creed

1. I believe in God the Father, Mak-er of the heav'n and earth,
2. Suf-fered un-der Pon-tius Pi-late, Cru-ci-fied for me he died;
3. At God's right hand he is seat-ed, till his com-ing as he said,
4. I be-lieve the Church of Je-sus forms one bod-y as a whole.

And in Je-sus Christ, our Sav-ior, God's own Son of match-less worth;
Laid with-in the grave so si-lent, gates of hell he o-pened wide.
Fi-nal judg-ment will be met-ed to the liv-ing and the dead,
All are one through-out the a-ges, with the saints I lift my soul.

Laid a-side his heav'n-ly glo-ry, By the Ho-ly Ghost con-ceived,
And the stone-sealed tomb was emp-ty, on the third day he a-rose,
I con-fess the Ho-ly Spir-it has been sent thru Christ the Son,
I be-lieve sins are for-giv-en, that our bod-ies will be raised;

Born un-to the Vir-gin Ma-ry, He in whom I have be-lieved.
In-to heav-en made his en-try, Might-y con-quer-or of his foes.
To ap-ply sal-va-tion's mer-it, God Al-might-y, Three in One.
Ev-er-last-ing life in heav-en, May God's ho-ly name be praised!

WORDS: Anonymous
MUSIC: Franz Joseph Haydn

The Nicene Creed

In some instances, congregations use the Nicene Creed rather than the Apostles' Creed to confess their faith. When we use this creed, we say:

We believe in one God,
   the Father, the Almighty,
   maker of heaven and earth,
   of all that is, seen and unseen.

We believe in one Lord, Jesus Christ,
   the only Son of God,
   eternally begotten of the Father,
   God from God, Light from Light,
   true God from true God,
   begotten, not made,
   of one Being with the Father;
   through him all things were made.
   For us and for our salvation
      he came down from heaven,
      was incarnate of the Holy Spirit and the Virgin
        Mary,
      and became truly human.
      For our sake he was crucified under Pontius Pilate;
      He suffered death and was buried.
      On the third day he rose again
      in accordance with the Scriptures;
      he ascended into heaven
      and is seated at the right hand of the Father.
      He will come again in glory
      to judge the living and the dead,
      and his kingdom will have no end.

We believe in the Holy Spirit, the Lord, the giver of life,
   who proceeds from the Father and the Son,
   who with the Father and the Son
      is worshiped and glorified,
   who has spoken through the prophets.
   We believe in the one holy catholic and apostolic
      church.
   We acknowledge one baptism
      for the forgiveness of sins.
   We look for the resurrection of the dead,
      and the life of the world to come. Amen.

Where Did It Come From?

The Nicene Creed, also called the Nicene-Constantinopolitan Creed, was the second major creed to be written by Christians. It resulted from the work of two ecumenical church councils. In A.D. 325, the Council at Nicea adopted it. In A.D. 381 the Council held in Constantinople expanded it. The articles of the creed arose at a time of debate about religious beliefs. People argued about the nature and relation of God, Jesus Christ, and the Holy Spirit.[4]

The response to the debate resulted in an emphasis in the Nicene Creed on God's oneness. This emphasis was to exclude any consideration of three Gods when we profess our belief in the Trinity, which includes God, Jesus Christ, and the Holy Spirit. It affirms the three divine persons who make up the one God, who is also known as the triune God. By A.D. 1014, the Nicene Creed was a regular part of the Roman Mass on Sundays and at festivals.

The Nicene Creed uses the plural "we" throughout, as opposed to the singular "I" found in the Apostles' Creed. "We" was used to emphasize the social character of our faith as a Christian community. The creed is a community statement, whereas the "I" in the Apostles' Creed emphasizes our individual profession of faith to the others in community.

How to Use the Song

The song that follows highlights three key ideas in the Nicene Creed: One God, One Faith, One Baptism. When we present this song in the church school, begin by giving the historical material indicated above. We may ask groups to hold a second "council" meeting. As part of the meeting, do the following:

- Recite the Nicene Creed as it appears in the spoken version. Then recite the words of the song and learn to sing the song.
- Explore the importance of the word "one" as it appears in the spoken creed and the song. Engage in this discussion and explore the remaining activities in small units of three to four persons. Ask each unit to choose a unit leader and a recorder. Ask the recorder to write the unit's responses on newsprint or paper in preparation for reporting back to the whole group.
- Discuss how the words "one Faith" in the song may relate to the spoken creed.
- Share your experiences of baptism, either your own or that of family members, and discuss why baptism is important in the Christian faith.
- Compare the content of the Nicene Creed with the content of the Apostles' Creed. Consider the preference of one over the other and why, if a preference exists.
- Discuss similarities and differences in the two songs.
- Consider why the Nicene Creed is still used in churches today. Also discuss the importance of the creed to how we live our everyday lives.
- Explore questions the Nicene Creed raises for you. Explore also some answers to the questions or suggest ways to get answers to the questions.
- Based on what you know about the Apostles' and Nicene Creeds, revise, using your own words, what you believe.
- Receive the reports from each unit. Then recite the Nicene Creed again and sing the song again.

We Believe in One True God

1. We be - lieve in one true God, Fa - ther, Son, and Ho - ly Ghost,
2. We be - lieve in Je - sus Christ, Son of God and Ma - ry's Son,
3. We con - fess the Ho - ly Ghost, who from both for - e'er pro - ceeds;

ev - er pres - ent help in need, praised by all the heaven - ly host;
who de - scend - ed from his throne and for us sal - va - tion won;
who up - holds and com - forts us in all tri - als, fears, and needs.

by whose might - y power a - lone all is made and wrought and done.
by whose cross and death are we res - cued from sin's mis - er - y.
Blest and Ho - ly Trin - i - ty, praise for - ev - er be to thee.

WORDS: Tobias Clausnitzer; trans. by Catherine Winkworth
MUSIC: J. G. Werner's *Choralbuch*; arr. by William H. Havergal

The Gloria Patri

The Gloria Patri (Glory Be to the Father) is used as an act of praise in Christian worship. Although it is sometimes spoken, it is most often sung. We recognize it by the words:

> Glory be to the Father, and to the Son,
>   and to the Holy Ghost;
> As it was in the beginning, is now,
>   and ever shall be, world without end.
>   AMEN.

Where Did the Gloria Patri Come From?

Reciting or singing the Gloria Patri is one of the oldest acts of Christian praise. The first part perhaps dates as far back as the second century. The second part was added sometime prior to the sixth century.[5] Its emphasis on three divine persons (Father, Son, and Holy Spirit) united in one Supreme Divine Being has basis in Scripture (Matt. 12:32; 28:19; Luke 12:10; Acts 2:33; 1 Cor. 12:4-6; 2 Cor. 13:14).

The Gloria Patri was sung by martyrs in the Roman Coliseum during the days of persecution in early Christendom. It also became part of the Christian community's praise response after the psalms, prayers, or sermons in worship services. By the nineteenth century, it was part of worship throughout the Christian world. It remains so today. One musical version used today was written by Charles Meineke in 1844. He was a German immigrant to the United States who served for many years as pianist and organist at St. Paul's Episcopal Church in Baltimore, Maryland. Another musical version was written by Henry Greatorex in 1851. He was an immigrant from England who served as organist at the Central Congregational Church in Hartford, Connecticut.[6]

The Gloria Patri has become known as the "Lesser Doxology" in comparison to the "Greater Doxology" called the Gloria in Excelsis Deo (Song of God's Glory).

Glory Be to the Father

WORDS: Lesser Doxology
MUSIC: Charles Meineke

Glory Be to the Father

WORDS: Lesser Doxology
MUSIC: Henry W. Greatorex

The Doxology

Doxology means "glory" or "utterance." The song we refer to as the Doxology, also called the "Great Doxology," is known as "Praise God From Whom All Blessings Flow." It is among the most frequently sung hymns of praise to God in Christian churches, past and present. Often, we sing it as a response to God after giving and presenting gifts.

We recognize the Doxology in its entirety by the words:

Praise God, from whom all blessings flow;
Praise God, all creatures here below;
Praise God above, ye heavenly host;
Praise Father, Son, and Holy Ghost. Amen.

Where Did the Doxology Come From?

The words of the Doxology were written by Thomas Ken in 1674. At the time he wrote them, Ken was chaplain to the bishop of Winchester Cathedral in England. The words actually make up the last verse of three hymns—one for morning, one for evening, and one for midnight services—Ken wrote for the boys at Winchester College.[7]

Like the Gloria Patri, the use of the Doxology in Christian worship has a basis in Scripture. In Old Testament times, the doxology was a formula for expressing praise to God. Examples of these blessings are found at the ends of hymns (1 Chron. 16:36; Ps. 41:13; 72:18-19; 106:48). In the early Christian church, the formula for the Doxology included God, through Jesus Christ (Rom. 16:27).

The oldest hymn tune, to which Ken's verse is set, was written by Louis Bourgeois. It was published in Geneva in 1551. Since then, the Doxology has been set to many other tunes.[8]

Praise God, from Whom All Blessings Flow

WORDS: Thomas Ken
MUSIC: Attr. to Louis Bourgeois

Advent Is the Season
(A Song of the Christian Year)

1. ___ Ad - vent is the sea - son of wait - ing for Mes - si - ah,
2. ___ Christ - mas is the sea - son of wel - com-ing the Sav - ior,
3. E - piph - a - ny is the sea - son we think a - bout the Ma - gi,
4. ___ Lent is the sea - son of pray - ing for for - give - ness,
5. ___ Eas - ter is the sea - son of great - est joy and glad - ness!
6. ___ Pen - te - cost is the sea - son the Church came in - to be - ing.

light - ing Ad - vent can - dles, and know - ing Christ is near. We
Je - sus in a man - ger, a babe of poor - est birth. We
bright - ly shin - ing star, and the gifts fit for a King, Christ's
grow - ing as dis - ci - ples, and giv - ing to the poor. We
Je - sus is a - live! No long - er is he dead! The
It was born the day that the Ho - ly Spir - it came. The

hear the words of proph - ets spo - ken to the peo - ple, "Pre -
think a - bout the shep - herds and the host of an - gels
bap - ti - sm by John, the mir - a - cle at Ca - na. "Em -
think of Je - sus' life, his fast - ing in the des - ert, the
stone was rolled a - way from the tomb where he was bur - ied.
Word of God was preached to man - y diff - 'rent peo - ples.

pare the way of God. "Christ will soon be here."
prais - ing God and say - ing, "Peace to all on earth."
man - u - el is with us," gifts of praise we bring.
pain - ful cru - ci - fix - ion he knew he must en - dure.
"Je - sus is not here! He has ris - en as he said."
Thou - sands in the crowd be - lieved on Je - sus' name.

WORDS and MUSIC: Nylea L. Butler-Moore

The Psalter

The Psalter includes the 150 psalms found in the Old Testament book called the Psalms that people of God throughout the world sing.

Where Did the Psalter Come From?

The psalter was the hymnal used at the Temple in Jerusalem. Often called the songs of David, the psalter we see in the Bible today results from the assembling together of parts of many collections of psalms.

The early Christians used psalms at communal gatherings, including meal times. Sometimes individuals sang psalms for others to hear without any response. At other times the listeners responded with a refrain after particular verses of a psalm.[9]

By the fourth century, churches included psalms as a standard part of worship. Christianity had gained respectability. Persecution of Christians had ceased. By that century's end, Christians were encouraged to come together every day, morning and evening, to sing psalms and pray in the chief church of a city. People opened the day with psalms. Through the psalms, they received God's Word. They gave thanks and praised God for the new day and new life in Jesus Christ.

People also closed each day by singing psalms to receive God's Word and to give thanks and praise to God for getting them through the day. Churches chose the psalms that suited their purposes of receiving God's Word and praying prayers of thankfulness and praise.[10]

In the fourth-century churches, people sang the psalms responsively. A leader, called a cantor, sang the verses. The congregation responded with a refrain, either using the word *Alleluia* or a phrase or verse from the psalm. This early use of the psalms, along with prayer by the people in churches formed a "cathedral" or "people's tradition."

In the fifth century, a monastic tradition developed. In this tradition, monks sang the psalms. They believed God was pleased to hear them and was glorified in this way. Their use of the psalter took place apart from the community life of the church. Over a given period of time, choirs of clergy in monasteries sang the entire psalter in the order they appear in the Bible. Other monks sang responses to each psalm using selected verses.

By the thirteenth century, the use of the psalms by clergy in monastic life developed into a "choral tradition" that was carried out in churches. In this tradition, two clergy choirs sang the verses alternately (called antiphonal singing). Before and after the choirs sang, the congregation sang a refrain (called an antiphon).

By the sixteenth century, the monastic and choral traditions overtook the "cathedral" or "people's tradition" as it was originally carried out. However, Protestant Reformers worked to recover the "people's tradition" by proposing uses of the psalter and prayer along with scripture teaching in churches, church groups, families, and community gatherings.[11] The recovery of the "people's tradition" blossomed in the sixteenth and seventeenth centuries. It laid the foundation for the central use of psalms, prayers, hymn-singing and scripture teaching in worship, class meetings, Bible study groups, and church schools in early American and today's churches.

By singing psalms as part of what we do with our church groups, we open the word of God to inspire and sustain them. We also offer them a way of praising God, entering into conversation with God by using the psalmist's words, and exploring the meaning of the psalms.

How to Use the Songs

The following songs are musical arrangements of psalms. These songs reflect four of the themes found in the psalter: invitation, praise, thanks, and declaration. Some general guidelines for using the songs include the following in addition to using the activities listed under each song:

- Invite group members to read the psalm in the Bible and identify its theme. A leader or several group members may begin the psalm and read every other verse, with the remaining group members responding to alternate verses.
- Ask group members to reflect on meanings the psalm holds for them.
- Speak the words of the song and then sing it to become familiar with it.
- Compare the words of the song with the words of the psalm as it appears in the Bible. Determine the similarities and differences. Also discuss the feelings, attitudes, and responses generated by the musical arrangement of the psalm.

Come! Come! Everybody Worship!

WORDS and MUSIC: Natalie Sleeth
© 1991 by Cokesbury.

Activities

1. Have the group learn the song. Have group members read aloud Psalm 95:1-7. Call attention to the theme of invitation in verses 1 and 2, and the theme of prayer in verse 6. Discuss the qualities that form the invitation and prayer. Have them identify who is being invited and what the nature of the invitation is.

2. Invite group members to read aloud the words of the refrain of the musical arrangement of the psalm. Ask them to compare verse 1 appearing in the musical version to Exodus 20:8, and verse 5 to Psalm 27:1.

3. Make individual greeting cards from construction paper, each showing one of the following phrases on the outside cover:
   Come! Everybody Worship!
   Come! Worship God!
   Worship and Remember
   God Is Like a Light

Decorate the outside covers of the greeting cards, write additional messages on the inside to send to potential members of your group, to members who have been absent for awhile, or to sick and shut-in members and friends.

A Song of Praise

Clap Your Hands

WORDS: Psalm 47: 1-2, 6-7 (adapted)
MUSIC: Anne Streaty Wimberly

all the earth. Sing prais - es with a psalm.

CLAP

Clap! Clap! Clap your hands! Clap your hands and

shout for joy. Clap! Clap! Clap your hands! Sing

prais - es with a psalm. Let all sing psalm.

Activities

1. Read Psalm 47:1-2, 6-7. Then read the words of the song.

2. Invite discussion by asking: "Why do we praise God? What are various ways we give praise to God?"

Clap Your Hands
Descant

Clap! Clap! Clap! Clap! Shout! Shout songs of joy.

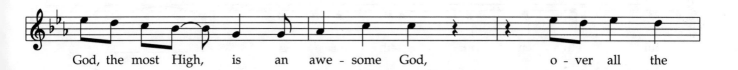

God, the most High, is an awe - some God, o - ver all the

earth. Let all sing prais - es! Sing prais-es to our God! Praise to

God. For God is o - ver all the earth.

Praise! Praise with a psalm. Clap! Clap! Clap your hands!

Clap your hands and shout for joy. Clap! Clap!

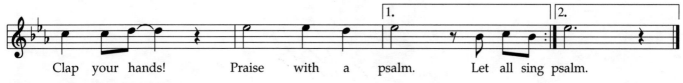

Clap your hands! Praise with a psalm. Let all sing psalm.

DESCANT: Anne Streaty Wimberly

A Song of Thanks

O Give Thanks

①
O give thanks, O give thanks, O give thanks un -

*
② to the Lord, for he is gra - cious and his mer - cy en -

dur - eth, en - dur - eth for - ev - er._____

*When sung as a grace, Group 1 sings through once and from the beginning to * again, while Group 2 (coming in at 2) sings through once.

WORDS and MUSIC: Traditional

Activities

1. Identify the theme of thanks appearing in the song.

2. Read Psalm 136:1-3. Then read the words of the song.

3. Sing the song as a prayer.

4. Invite discussion by asking: "What are the things for which we are thankful? What are various ways we give thanks to God?"

A Song of Declaration

The Lord's My Shepherd

1. The Lord's my Shepherd, I'll not want; He
2. My soul he doth re - store a - gain; And
3. Yea, though I walk in death's dark vale, Yet
4. My ta - ble thou hast fur - nish - ed In
5. Good - ness and mer - cy all my life Shall

makes me down to lie in pas - tures green; he
me to walk doth make With - in the paths of
will I fear no ill; For thou are with me,
pres - ence of my foes; My head thou dost with
sure - ly fol - low me; And in God's house for -

lead - eth me The qui - et wa - ters by.
righ - teous - ness, E'en for his own name's sake.
and thy rod and staff me com - fort still.
oil a - noint, And my cup o - ver - flows.
ev - er - more My dwell - ing place shall be.

WORDS: *Scottish Psalter* (Psalm 23)
MUSIC: William Havergal; arr. Lowell Mason
Music arr. © 1968 by Graded Press

Activities

1. Read aloud the words of the song. Then read silently the words of Psalm 23 in the Bible. Identify the theme of declaration. Note that in the song as in the psalm, the writer declares who God is and how God acts.

2. Invite group members to discuss the nature of the task of a shepherd and the qualities of a good shepherd. Also invite them to reflect on times they have relied on God as shepherd and what impact their awareness of God as shepherd had on them during those times.

3. Ask group members to close their eyes and image God's presence as shepherd in their home, workplace, school, church, and places of recreation while someone plays the musical arrangement of the psalm on the piano, or on an audiotape.

6. PRAY IN SONG

An Example

*T*he church families gathered on a Saturday for an all-day retreat planned by the family life ministry team. The retreat had been organized to bring families together for a day of learning, reflection, and fun. Their theme was "Families Praying, Families Playing." Along with periods of family games, the retreat experiences focused on what prayer is, ways families can enter into prayer, and occasions when this can happen.

They began the retreat with a prayer song. The retreat leader introduced the prayer song by saying that the best way for families to start the day is to connect together with the One who will guide us through the day. The leader then added that, in addition to individual prayer times, it is important for the whole family to intentionally include prayer songs or other approaches to prayer during a meal time and/or in the evening.

The leader described prayer as our ongoing conversation with God as we go about our daily lives. The leader gave examples of entering this conversation by using the psalms, by praying the prayer Jesus taught his disciples, by reading prayers someone had already written, by writing our own prayers, and by speaking spontaneous prayers. The leader also said that family prayer has to be intentionally planned and that a helpful way for families to enter into prayer was to sing them as they had done to open the retreat.

The participants then formed small family clusters representing different ages/stages. They shared their own songs, approaches to and times of family prayer, and prayed for one another. They also shared prayers they had learned and stories about who taught them. Reporters from the clusters summarized for the whole group what they did and learned in the clusters. The whole group learned several prayer songs. The experiences focused on prayer ended with meetings of the individual family units. The families developed a "prayer covenant" in which they made a pledge to pray together at a specific time or times each day. They also included in their covenant the statements of individual family members on why they considered it important to pray together.

What It Means to Pray in Song

Praying in song is an important part of our religious heritage. Today, as in past times, people approach God in song with messages of the heart when ordinary spoken language seems inadequate. We approach God's presence and welcome God in song. Through song, we connect with the welcoming Spirit of God and enter into spiritual communion with God, who has already invited us and is already listening.

When we enter our conversations with God through song, we may sing the psalms as prayers. We may sing the prayer Jesus taught his disciples. We may sing praises to God in song. We may thank God in song. We may pour out our grief and make an appeal to God to act. We may ask God for guidance through song. We may commit ourselves to God and seek God's benediction or blessing through song.

In prayer songs, we are free to repeat our thoughts and feelings without concern for stuttering. The rhythm allows us to emphasize key words and syllables to impress upon the heart of God what is of great significance to us. Through the rise and fall of melody, we reveal the character of the stories that make up our conversation with God. And, with every silence, we show that we are not simply singing a prayer, but we are also breathing a prayer and listening to God.

Prayer songs are prayers in and of themselves. But, we also use them along with other forms of prayers. They are means of entering periods of spoken prayer and silent meditation for individuals and groups. Through prayer songs, we enter into a prayerful attitude and begin to form our prayer language. We also use prayer songs to help bring to a close periods of spoken prayer and silent meditation. Prayer songs heighten our awareness of being in God's presence.[1]

When we invite our groups to sing prayer songs, we foster their learning more about what it means to enter into conversation with God. By singing prayer songs, we actually provide important opportunities for them to enter this conversation. Moreover, we show them ways to begin and end times of spoken and silent prayer.

How to Make It Happen

A number of prayer songs appear in the preceding chapters. Take some time to review these songs with groups. Use the songs as spoken prayers. Sing them as prayers. Begin and end times of spoken prayer with the songs. The songs, song function, and the chapters in which to find them are as follows:

Name of the Prayer Song	Function	Chapter
"Jesu, Jesu"	Guidance	2
"May the Lord, Mighty God"	Blessing	3
"Many and Great, O God"	Praise	3
"Kum Ba Yah"	God's presence	3
"Dear Lord, Lead Me Day by Day"	Guidance	3
"Daw-Kee, Aim Daw-Tsi-Taw"	Appeal to God	3
"The Lord's Prayer"	Appeal to God	5
"O Give Thanks"	Thanksgiving	5

Use the prayer songs that follow in similar ways. Call attention to the potential use of the songs by individuals and by families. Also, use the suggested activities indicated below each song.

Good Morning, God

Good morn - ing God, Good morn - ing God! I thank you for this day. Good

morn - ing God, Good morn - ing God! I real - ly want to say: Thank you.

I'm hap - py! I'm glad! I'm joy - ful, not sad! I'm

up! I'm here! I'm sing- ing to make it clear:

WORDS and MUSIC: Anne Streaty Wimberly
© 1996 Abingdon Press

Activities

1. Before singing the song, ask group members to list all the things for which they are thankful. Ask them to explore how and when they can express their thanks to God. Also discuss ways of addressing God and beginning a prayer of thanks at different times during the day.

2. Call attention to the function of the words as giving thanks to God. Create spoken prayers of thanks to God.

3. Have children draw pictures of the things for which they are thankful. Invite them to describe their pictures. After each description, ask all group members to respond with "Thank you, God."

The Lord's Prayer

WORDS: Matthew 6:9-13; adapt. by J. Jefferson Cleveland and Verolga Nix
MUSIC: West Indian folk tune; arr. by Carlton R. Young

Activities

1. Read Matthew 6:9-13.

2. For discussion, ask: "When did you first learn the Lord's Prayer? From whom did you learn it? In what places and under what circumstances do you now say it? What does this prayer mean to you?"

3. Describe this prayer as the model prayer for Christians.

4. Call attention to the West Indian origin of this musical arrangement of the Lord's Prayer.

Lord, I Want to Be a Christian

1. Lord, I want to be a Chris-tian In-a my heart, in-a my heart,
2. Lord, I want to be more lov-ing In-a my heart, in-a my heart,
3. Lord, I want to be more ho-ly In-a my heart, in-a my heart,
4. Lord, I want to be like Je-sus In-a my heart, in-a my heart,

Lord, I want to be a Chris-tian In-a my heart.
Lord, I want to be more lov-ing In-a my heart.
Lord, I want to be more ho-ly In-a my heart.
Lord, I want to be like Je-sus In-a my heart.

In-a my heart, In-a my heart,
In-a my heart, In-a my heart,

Lord, I want to be a Chris-tian In-a my heart.
Lord, I want to be more lov-ing In-a my heart.
Lord, I want to be more ho-ly In-a my heart.
Lord, I want to be like Je-sus In-a my heart.

WORDS and MUSIC: Afro-American spiritual

Activities

1. Before singing the song as a prayer, invite the group to explore what influences people's desire to become Christian. Ask: "What are the qualities that Christians should exhibit? What is meant by the Christian lifestyle?" Make a list of the responses.

2. Have group members read Romans 12:9-14 and Galatians 5:22-26. Invite discussion on the following: "What qualities of Christians did you find in the scripture? What characteristics of the Christian lifestyle did you find?" Compare the characteristics found in scripture with the group's list of responses. Add to the list anything found in scripture that is not included there.

3. Invite the group to read the first line of every verse. Ask: "What is significant about the words, 'In my heart?'" Sing the song as a prayer.

Just a Closer Walk with Thee

Slow for refrain, spiritually for chorus

WORDS and MUSIC: Traditional

Activities

1. Invite discussion by asking the following: "What are some of the difficulties we as human beings face in our daily lives? Do Christians lead trouble-free lives? Why? How may we get through hard times?"

2. Read: Romans 8:35-39; James 1:5-6.

3. Ask individual group members to read the verses and the entire group to sing the refrain. Then sing the entire prayer song.

4. Use the refrain as a group response to sentence prayers.

Jesus, Remember Me

Je - sus, re - mem-ber me when you come in - to your king - dom.

Je - sus, re - mem-ber me when you come in - to your king - dom.

WORDS: Luke 23:42
MUSIC: Jacques Berthier and the Community of Taizé

Music © 1981 Les Presses de Taizé, by permission of G.I.A. Publications, Inc.

Activities

1. Read Luke 23:32-42, with particular emphasis on verse 42. Then sing the song.

2. To invite discussion, ask: "For what reasons would you want to be remembered by Jesus? What is the nature of the kingdom mentioned in the song?"

7. EIGHT WAYS TO TEACH NEW SONGS

When we invite a group to sing a song, we often ask how many already know the song. When many group members answer in the affirmative, we know that the group will sing the song with less effort than it would take if no one knew it. But, what if nearly all, if not all, of the group members say that they have never heard the song we have chosen? How may we go about teaching unfamiliar songs? In this chapter, we will explore eight ways of teaching new songs.

1. Use Commercially Recorded Music

There is an abundance of recorded religious music of various styles that may be purchased for use with church groups. Whether on tape or compact disc (CD), recorded music offers groups the opportunity to listen to both the words and melody of a song and to sing along often with the benefit of accompaniments.

When using commercially recorded music as a method for teaching new songs, determine if the song you wish to teach appears in the church hymnal or other available books or materials. A group will find it easier to learn a song they are hearing, particularly if it is lengthy, if they can see a version of the song that closely approximates the recorded one.

When written materials are not available, and the song is short, is easy to follow or is repetitive, invite the group to listen to it first. Then invite the group to hum along with the music, and finally, invite them to sing along with the recorded music. If the song is lengthy or has complicated melody, rhythm, and/or words, invite the group to learn the song using the following sequence:

- Listen to the recorded music.
- Hum along with the recorded music.
- Recite the words of the refrain or chorus, when there is one.
- Sing the refrain or chorus when it occurs during the replay of the recorded music.
- Recite the words of the verses, one at a time.
- Sing each verse when it occurs during the replay of the recorded music.
- Sing the whole song along with the recorded music.

Whenever using copyrighted materials, it is important to honor the copyright law as it appears on the materials. This includes any written materials from hymn books or other songbooks. These materials must not be duplicated for group use unless permission is acquired to do so.

2. Use Music Recorded by Church Musicians

Leaders/teachers may use to great advantage the expertise of church musicians. Choir director, choirs, and individual musicians may be called upon to record songs that are desired for use with a group. Taped versions of songs done by these musicians may be introduced in the manner stated above. These musicians may also agree to come into your group session to teach the song(s) you would like to use to enhance your group's experience.

When we recruit church musicians to teach songs to our groups, it is important that we share with them the purpose for using the song(s). It is helpful if they know in advance, for example, if our intent is to sing songs to build community, to affirm music as a gift of various cultures, to tell a Bible story, to teach about a particular church tradition, or to teach about prayer.

Moreover, the church musician who agrees to teach songs to our groups should be told how many songs are needed and if the song(s) should be presented as an opener to the group's time together, or in conjunction with a study topic or Bible passage, or for a closing experience. If any songs are to be correlated with a study topic or Bible passage, specific information about the topic or Bible passage and their use will need to be shared with the church musician.

We may meet with the church musician to suggest or review possible songs and to show the musician songs we may like to use that already appear in the group's study materials. We may also leave the choice of the song(s) entirely up to the church musician after giving him or her the information already discussed and if he or she agrees to do so.

3. Use Talented Members of the Group

We may seek the leadership of group members who have musical backgrounds and who, as a result, sing well or play instruments. As in the case of our use of church musicians, recruited group members also need to know the purpose of the music they will teach. Consequently, it is helpful if they know in advance, the information presented above that we would share with church musicians. Also, as in the case of our use of church musicians, we may meet with recruited leaders from our groups to suggest or review possible songs, especially when songs already appear in study materials being used in a group session. We may also leave the choice of songs entirely up to recruited leaders if the leader is amenable and has the ability to do so.

Often children and youth who have become accomplished in singing or playing an instrument enjoy "teaming up" or forming an ensemble to teach songs to their peers. These recruits from the group are called "teaching ensembles." They may also elect to record their ensemble version of a song for use in teaching their peers. Of course, we may encourage adult recruits who desire to form "teaching ensembles" to do so and to record their ensemble versions of a song they have agreed to teach to their peers.

4. Combine with Other Church School Groups

An enjoyable and helpful way to learn new songs in the church school is to allow a group to hear what another group is singing and to learn songs from them. When we do this, we allow our church school group to "catch" some of the excitement other groups have in singing revered songs and songs that have added to their understanding of the gospel.

Times of sharing songs also offer an opportunity for a group to verbally recount in the presence of another group meanings a song holds for them. This might include the circumstances under which they learned and sang the song as part of their group experience. This kind of sharing enhances the teaching/learning process and appreciation for others' musical tastes.

5. Teach Songs Using the All-Join-In Method

When we have some musical proficiency and feel comfortable teaching new songs to our groups, we may choose to do so in a variety of ways. One of those ways is through the all-join-in method. This method is typically used when a song is relatively short in length and is simply written as indicated by its repeated words, rhythm, and/or melody. To use this method, we invite the group to listen once or twice as we sing the entire song. We may or may not use accompaniment as we sing. If we do, we may use the piano, a guitar, an autoharp, or bells. We then invite the group to join in singing the song in its entirety.

"I'm Goin'a Sing When the Spirit Says Sing" appears in chapter 1. Teach this song using the all-join-in method. Use the method and the song with every age/stage group. Sing the song with or without accompaniment. The song may also be taught by a church musician, or a talented member of the group, or with other church school groups who already know the song. Practice the all-join-in approach with this song and other short songs appearing in the earlier chapters.

6. Teach Songs Using the Whole-Part-Whole Method

When a song is made up of verses and a refrain, it is helpful to invite the group to listen to the whole song. When we sing the song a second time, we invite the group to join in with only the refrain of the song. By singing only the refrain, the group has the opportunity to hear the message, melody, and rhythm of the verses enough times to create familiarity and ease when they finally sing the whole song.

The refrain of the following song, "Go, Tell It on the Mountain" appears in chapter 3. Teach the entire song using the whole-part-whole method. In this song, the refrain is set at the beginning. Therefore, we would begin singing the refrain followed by the entire song before continuing with the whole-part-whole process just described. Teach the song, using this method, to all age groups, with the exception of young children. Young children may be invited to sing only the refrain while the leader/teacher and/or older age groups continue singing the verses. The song may also be taught by a church musician, or a talented member of a group, or with other church school groups. Practice the whole-part-whole approach with this song.

Go, Tell It on the Mountain

WORDS: John W. Work, Jr. (Lk. 2:8-20)
MUSIC: Afro-American spiritual; adapt. and arr. by William Farley Smith

Adapt. and arr. © 1989 The United Methodist Publishing House

7. Teach Songs Using the Phrase-wise Couplet Method

We help groups to learn lengthy or musically challenging songs when we teach them using the phrase-wise couplet method. First, sing to the group the entire song, with or without accompaniment, while the group listens, in order to familiarize them with the song's message and sound. Then proceed with the phrase-wise couplet teaching method. In this method we present two phrases at a time. We begin with the first of two phrases followed by the second phrase. We then invite the group to sing the two phrases one after the other. We present all of the subsequent phrases of the song in this fashion. An example of a song to teach using the phrase-wise couplet method is "Didn't My Lord Deliver Daniel," which appears in chapter 4. Use the steps of this method as they appear on the following pages.

Sing the following in its entirety:

Didn't My Lord Deliver Daniel

Did-n't my Lord de - liv - er Dan — iel, de - li - ver Dan — iel, de - liv - er Dan — iel?

Did-n't my Lord de - liv - er Dan — iel, And why not - a ev - e - ry — one?

He de - liv - er'd Dan - iel from the li - on's den, Jo - nah from the bel - ly of the

whale, and the He - brew chil - dren from the fie - ry fur - nace, And why not ev - e - ry - one?

Invite the group to listen to phrase 1 and then sing it.

Invite the group to listen to phrase 2 and then sing it.

Invite the group to sing phrases 1 and 2.

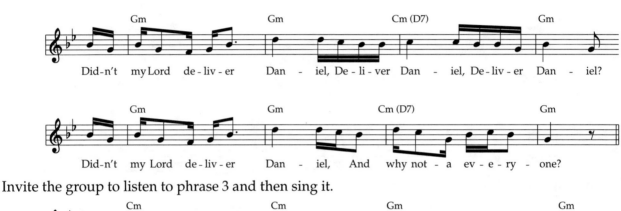

Invite the group to listen to phrase 3 and then sing it.

Invite the group to listen to phrase 4 and then sing it.

Invite the group to sing phrases 3 and 4.

Invite the group to listen to all four phrases and then sing them.

94

8. Help Groups Follow Verses

We help to enhance people's enjoyment of music both within and outside the group when we take time to guide them through the verses of songs.

We cannot take for granted that children, youth, and adults follow multiple verses of unfamiliar songs with ease. With this in mind, we may help them follow verses by using two key aids. The first aid consists of inviting group members to read each verse aloud. Stop at the end of each phrase or line of every verse. As leaders/teachers, we may call out the word that begins the next phrase or line and make sure that every group member has found it. Or, we may ask group members to call out the word that begins the next line as a way of confirming their finding it. At the end of each verse, we will want to make sure that everyone has found the beginning point of the subsequent verse.

The second aid is to number the verses throughout the song, or when teaching songs with multiple verses to elementary-age readers, use contrasting emblems or colors to identify each verse. To do this, we will need to have music books and hymnals especially for their use. The following song from chapter 2, "Jesu, Jesu," shows how to use both aids. The verses are numbered throughout. A star identifies verse 1. A circle identifies verse 2. A square identifies verse 3. A triangle identifies verse 4. A wavy line identifies verse 5.

Jesu, Jesu

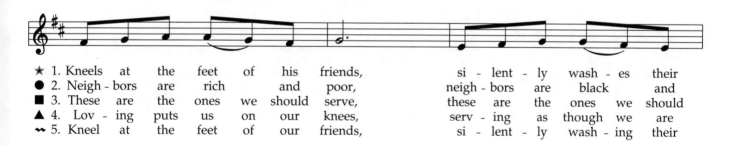

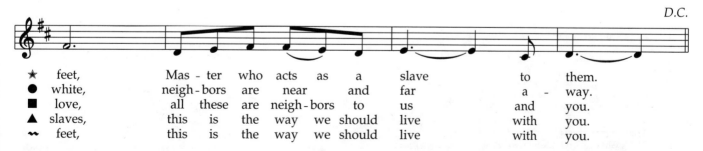

WORDS: Tom Colvin
MUSIC: Ghana folk song; adapt. by Tom Colvin; arr. by Charles H. Webb

NOTES

1. Sing for Joy

1. This creation story is found in Mary Batchelor, *The Children's Bible* (Belleville, Mich.: Lion Publishing Corp., 1985), 10.

2. Sing Songs to Build Community

1. Whitemore, Carol. *Symbols of the Church* (Nashville: Abingdon Press, 1987).
2. Mary Batchelor, *The Children's Bible* (Belleville, Mich.: Lion Publishing Corp., 1985).
3. Kenneth Cain Kinghorn, *Discovering Your Spiritual Gifts: A Personal Inventory Method* (Grand Rapids, Mich.: Francis Asbury Press, 1981).

3. Sing Songs from Many Cultures

1. Harold M. Best, *Music Through the Eyes of Faith* (San Francisco: Harper San Francisco, 1993), 65, 67.
2. Ibid., 67-68.
3. Anne Streaty Wimberly and Edward Wimberly, *Language of Hospitality: Intercultural Relations in the Household of God* (Nashville: The United Methodist Church General Board of Discipleship, Division of Church School Publications, 1991).
4. M. Franklin Dotts, ed., *Building a New Community: God's Children Overcoming Racism* (Nashville: Church School Publications, 1992).

4. Tell Bible Stories Through Song

1. A song sung at Bible study and prayer fellowship, Ghana, West Africa, typically sung in Ewe, the general language in the Volta region of Ghana. Translated and sung by Dorothy Akota to Anne Wimberly, 1993. Notated by Anne Wimberly, 1993.

5. Tell About Church Traditions Through Song

1. Theodore W. Jennings, *Loyalty to God: The Apostles' Creed in Life and Liturgy* (Nashville: Abingdon Press, 1992), 15.
2. Peter G. Cobb, "The Liturgy of the Word in the Early Church," in *The Study of Liturgy*, ed. Cheslyn Jones, Geoffrey Wainwright, and Edward Yarnold (New York: Oxford University Press, 1978), 187.
3. Maxie Dunham, *This Is Christianity* (Nashville: Abingdon Press, 1994), 12.
4. For more information see Marianne H. Micks, *Loving the Questions: An Exploration of the Nicene Creed* (Valley Forge, Pa.: Trinity Press International, 1993).
5. H. Augustine Smith, *Lyric Religion: The Romance of Immortal Hymns* (New York: Fleming H. Revell Company, 1931), 110-11.
6. Ibid., 112.
7. William J. Reynolds, *Songs of Glory* (Grand Rapids, Mich.: Zondervan Publishing House, 1990), 227.
8. H. Augustine Smith, *Lyric Religion*, 338.
9. Paul F. Bradshaw, *Two Ways of Praying* (Nashville: Abingdon Press, 1995), 76.
10. Robert Taft, *The Liturgy of the Hours in East and West* (Collegeville, Minn.: Liturgical Press, 1986), 56.
11. James F. White, *Introduction to Christian Worship*, rev. ed. (Nashville: Abingdon Press, 1990), 130-31.

6. Pray in Song

1. See Margaret M. Poloma and George H. Gallup, *Varieties of Prayer: A Survey Report* (Philadelphia: Trinity Press International, 1992).

RESOURCES

The following materials and resources are suggested for use as aids in preparing for and implementing suggested activities found throughout the book.

Rhythm Band Instruments. Rhythm Band, Inc., Harris Music Publications, P.O. Box 1356, Fort Worth, TX 76101. Also available in Cokesbury stores.

First Note Melody Bells. Trophy Music Company, Cleveland, OH 44113. Also available in Cokesbury stores.

The Native Americans. A six-part series by TBS Productions, Inc., One CNN Center, Atlanta GA 30303.

We All Came to America. Republic Pictures Home Video, #7935. Post-Newsweek Productions, 12636 Beatrice St., Los Angeles, CA 90066-0930.

Island of Hope—Island of Tea: The Story of Ellis Island and The American Immigration Experience. Guggenheim Productions, Inc., Washington, D.C.

A Woman Called Moses: Life Story of Harriet Ross Tubman. Xenon Video, Inc. #XE XSR 1026, distributed by Xenon Entertainment, Santa Monica, CA.

Roots: The Lineage of One Family. Six episodes. Warner Home Video, 4000 Warner Blvd., Burbank, CA 91522.

Roots: The Next Generation. Seven episodes. Warner Home Video, 4000 Warner Blvd., Burbank, CA 91522.

Martin Luther King, Jr.: An Amazing Grace. Roots of the black peace movement from the 1955 bus boycott in Montgomery, Alabama to the "I Have a Dream" speech at the Washington Monument. Xenon Home Video Production, Santa Monica, CA.

INDEX OF SONGS